SO-BAO-207

155.5   R503116
Coh   12.95
Cohen   May90
Coping with sibling rivalry

DATE DUE			
JE 26 '90			
AG 06 '90			
MY 14 '9			
AG 08 '9			
NO 03 '94			
FE 14 '95			

BR

GREAT RIVER REGIONAL LIBRARY
St. Cloud, Minnesota   56301

COPING WITH

Sibling Rivalry

Shari Cohen

ROSEN PUBLISHING GROUP, INC./NEW YORK

R503116

345 9138

Published in 1989 by The Rosen Publishing Group, Inc.
29 East 21st Street, New York, NY 10010

Copyright 1989 by Shari Cohen

All rights reserved. No part of this book may be reproduced in any form
without permission in writing from the publisher, except by a reviewer.

First Edition

Library of Congress Cataloging-In-Publication Data

Cohen, Shari.
   Coping with sibling rivalry / Shari Cohen.—1st ed.
     p. cm.
   Bibliograpy: p.
   Includes index.
   Summary: Defines sibling rivalry and discusses how
it can manifest itself, how it affects the brothers and
sisters involved, and how it can be handled.
   ISBN 0-8239-0977-8 :
   1. Sibling rivalry—Juvenile literature.   [1. Sibling
rivalry. 2. Brothers and sisters.]   I. Title.
BF723.S43C64   1989
155.5—dc20   89-10305
                                  CIP
                                  AC

Manufactured in the United States of America

ABOUT THE AUTHOR ◇

Shari Cohen is a native of Minneapolis, Minnesota. She attended the University of Minnesota, where she majored in English and Journalism. In 1972 she moved to Los Angeles and began working for the federal government in the space program.

During that time she began working part time as a freelance writer, contributing human interest stories to newspapers and magazines nationwide.

In 1980 Shari Cohen began writing books for children and young adults. She is the author of the children's books *Macaroni and Fleas* and *Prime Time Rhyme*. She also wrote *Coping with Being Adopted* and *Coping with Failure* for the young-adult coping series of the Rosen Publishing Group. Her most recent project is a series of novels for handicapped young adults.

She now lives in Woodland Hills, California, with her husband, Paul, and three children, twins Adam and Stephanie, and Barry.

Contents

Introduction

During adolescence your sisters and brothers are a major part of your life, for better or worse. You can't disown them, divorce them, or wish them away. While many of your friends come and go, Your sisters and brothers are still your sisters and brothers no matter what. They have a profound impact on your own life and self-esteem.

The power of sibling relationships lasts far beyond the childhood years. It provides an important emotional security for most people in the later stages of life. You may not agree with this statement right now, however, if you are experiencing power struggles, resentments, and jealousies within your family circle.

Many of you may admit to a basic underlying love for your brother or sister but feel unable to cope with this person on a day-to-day basis. Perhaps you feel that someone else in the family is the "favored one." This feeling of favoritism not only is the basis of sibling rivalry but also affects your own feelings of self-worth. You may feel that no matter what you do or say you will never receive the love or recognition from your parents that you deserve.

In this book we will study these acts of favoritism. We will hear from experts in the field and from teens who are experiencing this type of situation in their everyday lives.

We will also look at the subject of birth order, where you stand in the family. Studies have shown that whether you were the firstborn, the second child, or the baby of the family has a big influence on what kind of conflicts you may be experiencing and what type of person you may turn out to be.

Too many hurt feelings and harsh words lately? Take time out to read these chapters. You may begin to understand the feelings that you carry toward your brother or sister. And once you understand the source of your feelings, you will be better able to handle the situations that arise.

CHAPTER 1

Inside the
Family Circle

The family is where it happens. Successes, failures, hopes, dreams, laughter, and tears are shared with the people we live with and care most about. In nurturing families, people confide secrets. They give spontaneous hugs and show their affection. Each member talks openly and listens with concern to how the other feels. It is a good feeling to know that we can turn to our family for comfort.

Within the family unit, there is also conflict. Parents fight, brothers and sisters fight. Harsh words are spoken and grudges held. But all of this is normal. Most families experience some degree of inner turmoil, sometimes on a daily basis.

Perhaps you feel that you live with too much conflict, too much arguing. You may imagine yourself living in a home where everyone is always happy and content, a home where people speak in soft voices and everyone agrees with everyone. In some families it is exactly like that. The atmosphere is polite. Everyone is respectful and pleasant. There are no outbursts of anger, no tearful hugs of reconciliation. Rooms are aways neat; meals are on time. Children do what is expected of them.

Although that may seem like an ideal place to be raised, it might surprise you to learn that in later years these family members often lose contact with one another. Brothers and sisters may go for years without hearing from each other. But think about it. What really is there to miss about these lost relationships? True feelings were never shared. There are no real emotional bonds or memories that would bring a person back.

Although you may feel that it would be wonderful to grow up in this perfect type of home setting, you should realize that intense feelings of love and hate are a part of human nature. It is healthy to voice differences of opinion. It is natural to become angry, to feel envy, to become hostile and anxious. When disagreements arise, many creative solutions can be worked out, especially in conflicts between brothers and sisters. Here are some examples:

- Being sensitive to the other's feelings.
- Approaching this person for a discussion of what happened, away from other family members.
- Admitting that what happened was your fault (if it was) and saying you are sorry.
- Explaining your feelings about the situation.
- Attempting to see the other side of the disagreement.
- Finding humor in the incident (if trivial).
- Accepting the other person's opinion, even though it may be different from your own.
- Being the first to "break the ice" if a grudge is prolonged.

Sometimes a solution does not have to be reached immediately. Just an acknowledgment of how the other person feels may be a breakthrough to a talk about the argument.

ACCEPTING DIFFERENCES

Michael, fifteen, and his ten-year-old brother, Bill, fought bitterly throughout each day. They argued about everything, from who drank the last glass of milk in the pitcher to what program to watch on TV. They were constantly in conflict. Michael considered Bill a pest: whiny, immature, and spoiled.

Then one afternoon Michael broke his leg during football practice. He was forced to hobble around on crutches for weeks. Bill came to his brother's assistance during this time. He opened doors for him, brought him his meals, and carried his books. Michael appreciated what Bill was doing for him and told him so. The two became closer. Michael began to realize that he had been too hard on his younger brother. He did not remember what it was like to be ten, liking skateboards, comics, and the things that ten-year-olds do. He expected Bill to think and feel the way he himself did. And when Bill showed lack of interest in Michael's activities, Michael became upset.

Michael apologized to Bill. He said that in the future he would try to respect Bill for what he was and how he felt about things that were important to him. Both brothers agreed to try to work things out between them in the future.

Most brothers and sisters have different interests, even if they have the same parents. Mindy likes to eat a full breakfast before leaving for school each morning. Her brother Brian prefers a quick glass of juice on his way out the door. Valerie enjoys going to horror movies with her friends on Saturday afternoon. Her sister Betty likes to stay home and watch the classics on TV. That's okay. People don't have to be alike. Each person has individual tastes— even identical twins. Although they may look exactly alike, they have individual preferences. It is important to realize that differences are constant, normal, healthy factors in any family.

Learning to live with other people's ways of thinking and acting takes patience and understanding. You may question your brother's sanity in liking to study lizards and snakes. Just the thought of it makes you shudder. It is easy to laugh at him, to tease him and roll your eyes at what he is doing. But try to see his side. He plans to make this subject his profession. His interests and hobbies lie in biology and the study of reptiles. You may think him odd for wanting to study snakes and lizards, but he is not odd at all. This is where his interest lies, not in music or art as your interests do.

Brothers and sisters often want the other to see and feel things the way they do. That is how most arguments originate. It is impossible to live in close contact with another person without experiencing feelings about your sibling, feelings such as:

- *Jealousy*—"He's more attractive than I am. He's more intelligent in most things, and he's better in sports. I feel inferior when I'm around him."
- *Resentment*—"She's more coordinated than I am in skating. We both like to skate but she outshines me, and I resent the attention she gets from everyone."
- *Anger*—"He doesn't respect my privacy. He goes out of his way to bug me. He looks through my closet and drawers and takes things without asking."

- *Guilt*—"My sister is shy and does not date much. I always feel bad when I have someplace to go on weekends and she stays home. Sometimes I feel like canceling my date because she doesn't have one."

Perhaps you can identify with the following:

Ann:	"I hate it when my older brother ignores me. He treats me as if I'm invisible, as if I'm not even there."
Mary:	"My sister is only a year younger than I, but she always gets everything first. Our parents consider her the 'baby' and it makes me feel left out."
Joanne:	"My three sisters always tease me when a boy calls asking for me. They want to know everything that was said. Sometimes I get so angry that I start screaming and hitting them. I wish they'd leave me alone."
Jeff:	"My brother is bigger and stronger than I am even though he is only fourteen and I am seventeen. He can overpower me in a fight. He knows this and likes to push me around."
Alexandra:	"There are six children in our family, three boys and three girls. I share a room with my two sisters. There is yelling and arguing in our house, but there is no place I can hide. I have no privacy. My sisters wear my clothes and use my personal things. I wish I was an only child."
Andrea:	"My sister always talks down to me, especially when she is around her friends.

If I ask her something, she becomes snobby and makes me feel stupid."

Robert: "My brother talks when I am trying to watch something on TV. He makes a lot of noise and then I start yelling at him and then my mother gets angry and makes me turn the TV off."

Paul: "I have an adopted brother who thinks he's better than me. He says that our parents are not his real parents and that he can do whatever he wants without following the rules of the house. We never go a day without an argument."

Sally: "My sister likes to hang around my friends, which makes me angry. She invites herself to go everywhere with us. She includes herself in on our plans even though she knows it makes me mad."

A VIEW FROM THE OTHER SIDE

As you can see, many different situations can bring about angry feelings and disagreements between brothers and sisters. Sometimes even a wrong expression or tone of voice can set people off on a round of fighting. Usually there is a reason behind the conflict and, of course, two sides to the story.

It is easy to sympathize with each of the young people who have just talked about their side. That is because we are hearing their interpretation of what is wrong in the relationship. Imagine for a moment that you could speak to the person on the other side, such as Paul's adopted brother or Joanne's three sisters. What do you think their complaints would be? Let's look into Andrea's family and see what her sister has to say about their differences.

Andrea's sister Lois, sixteen, was born with a mild form of dyslexia, a learning disability. She has always had problems with her schoolwork and has had to have special tutoring for as long as she can remember. Andrea is a straight A student. Her scholastic awards are displayed throughout the house. Lois feels that Andrea is the favored daughter in the family because of her successes in school. Lois feels the little girl in her wanting to strike out and hurt Andrea, admitting her jealousy. What she is feeling is—"You're the smarter one. Mom and Dad like you better. I'll never be as good as you in their eyes." But that is not the "adult" thing to say when you are sixteen. So she tries to hurt Andrea in the only way she knows how, by being cold and indifferent and talking down to her. In Lois's mind she is trying to be the better one. She secretly hopes that her attitude will make Andrea go away.

Let's take a look into Carl's family. His brother, Alan, delights in tattling on Carl's every move. It has been that way since they were young children. But now Carl is eighteen. Alan is sixteen and, according to Carl, making his life miserable.

Alan tells it differently. Carl is the good-looking one, he says. Carl is the one who always gets the dates, who always has a full social calendar. Alan feels that he has always walked in Carl's shadow, watching his brother do many of the things that he wanted to do. Alan admits that he is shy. He has little confidence in his own abilities. By telling their parents of Carl's activities, he is unconciously trying to get his brother in trouble. Many times it works and Carl is grounded. Alan feels that while he can't physically hold Carl back, he can do it in a roundabout way by going through their parents.

The little boy in Alan feels like saying—"Everyone likes you because you look and act better than I do. You are having all the fun and it's not fair. I'm going to make it so you'll have to stay home, just like me."

But Alan is not five years old. He is a young adult and expected to think and act like one. While pretending to be a loving brother, Alan is really attempting to undermine Carl. He does not want Carl to be better than he is, and he is reacting in the only way he knows how.

IT TAKES TWO

You've probably heard that expression. And so it does. How often have you heard an aunt or a cousin or a friend tell of an argument that they've had with another person? They rant and rave, saying—"This person said this and this person said that. Imagine the nerve of this person to say such a thing." And then *you* think what a terrible person that must be. *You* get mad at that person too, until one day you happen to hear the other side of the story. Suddenly, that person does not seem so awful at all. Could your aunt have been in the wrong? Did she say or do something that instigated the argument?

It always helps to step back and try to see the other person's side in a conflict. Listen to what he or she is saying. There may even be a hidden feeling behind a person's outburst or accusation. Sometimes it is a feeling that has been buried for years and is now brought to the surface by just a certain look or comment. How many of you have lost your cool with someone for no apparent reason, and after looking for an answer to your outburst realized that you were reacting to a hurt from the past that had long since been buried? You may be sorry or feel embarrassed for your reaction and try to cover it up.

It's not easy. Not everyone can step back and see the other side in a conflict, or take the initiative to look into their past for answers. There are other ways in which you can work to defuse a situation or begin to mend a valued relationship. Many times it takes an admission of feeling on your part. You can start by admitting:

- I never knew you felt that way...
- I didn't realize you would take it the the way you did...
- I would have acted differently had I known...
- I wish you had said something...
- I had no idea you were sensitive about the subject...
- I admit I was wrong. Can you forgive me?

As you know, when brothers and sisters become angry with each other, they often become immediately defensive in their position. By practicing some of the above methods, by allowing yourself to hear the other side, and by listening to what is really being said you open the pathway for better understanding and communication between you. Think it over. Try to see yourself as the other is seeing you. Is the other justified in his or her position? Ask yourself:

- Do I really have a tendency to brag?
- Do I really embarrass him in front of his friends?
- Have I been too pushy lately?

- Did I have a disregard for her property?
- Have I been acting abusive toward him or her?

SHUTTING OFF FEELINGS

Often when our own feelings are hurt we have a tendency to shut the other person out of our lives. That may be done in a number of ways: sulking, ignoring, avoiding eye contact, not speaking.

Let's say that your brother called you fat. You were hurt, insulted, and embarrassed because it was said in front of others. Now you are angry and have decided that you will shut him out of your life. For days you give your brother the silent treatment. He finally gives up trying to talk to you and goes his own way. The silence thickens. Weeks go by. The comment about being fat has long been forgotten. Now, you label him cold, unfeeling, unloving. He is angry too and refers to you as moody, unresponsive.

What if you had responded immediately to your feelings about being called fat? When the two of you were alone, you could have approached him and explained that he embarrassed you by his comment. You would in all probability have heard him respond either that he was only kidding or that he didn't realize you would take it the way you did. The two of you could have discussed it, and the subject could have been dropped.

By shutting off responses to a negative remark made to you, you open up the pathway for days or weeks of brooding or holding a grudge. Next time, make an attempt to respond immediately. The other person will not fall apart at your approach. He or she may be more flexible than you think.

Often we have to recognize a statement for what it really

is: a joke, a passing thought, an offhand remark, a seeking for attention from you, a voicing of concern.

Sometimes it helps to reassure a sibling that you love him or her and really want to work things out. Just a few words can begin to open up clogged lines of communication. You may not get immediate results. But try to realize that most brothers and sisters fight at one time or another. Your generation is not much different from that of your parents. It basically stems back to early childhood feelings that many of us still carry with us:

> *You* are loved the most...I want to be loved as you are.
>
> *You* are the prettier one...I wish I were as pretty as you.
>
> *You* are better in sports...I want to play ball as you do.
>
> *You* have more privileges...I want those privileges too.
>
> *You* get more attention from Mom and Dad...I want attention from them.

It was much easier to express these "I" feelings when you were younger. Clenched fists, stomping feet, pouting face often gave way to tearful tantrums. But then it was over and forgotten. Brooding about an argument or holding a grudge is something that we learn to do as we grow older.

At sixteen it becomes "uncool" to expose these childish feelings to others. At sixteen you have a new, different image to portray. Tears are often held back. True feelings are kept inside, and walls are put up to prevent emotions from coming through.

IMITATING ATTITUDES

It is difficult for some people, as adults, to show their true emotion. Pure excitement may come through only as a half smile. Sorrow may be reflected by a stone-sober expression. Fear may come across as just walking away from a situation. Many of these types of people came from homes in which tears were a sign of weakness. Some parents, in an effort to keep peace in the family, forbade fighting among the children and constantly reprimanded them for disagreeing with one another.

These children as adults still hold to those attitudes. They have learned to cover up their true feelings. Often they are thought of as cold or unfeeling, but underneath their feelings run deep. They would like to throw their arms around a loved one at the airport and say a tearful good-bye, but they can't. The way we were raised as children plays a major part in how we think and act as adults.

Brothers and sisters who were taught to compete early in life often find themselves competing long after they are out on their own. Sisters may argue bitterly about which has the better husband or family. Brothers may compete against each other in the business world. It isn't unusual to find a person competing with a sibling's memory long after that sibling has died.

The role that children play toward each other in the family circle in the early years carries through to how they relate as adults. Perhaps you are experiencing conflict with your brother or sister now, as a young adult. Think back to your earlier relationship. How did you get along then? Did you fight over toys? Do you fight now about makeup or clothes or the keys to the car?

It is important to realize that as a young adult you have alternative ways to handle these conflicts. Your parents are not always around to be mediators as they once were. You can begin by watching yourself and your reaction when a tense or hurtful situation arises.

- Pay attention to how you react when something hurtful is said to you by a sibling. Do you strike back immediately? Do you walk away?
- Notice your body stance. Are you tense? Are your hands clenched?
- Listen to the tone of your voice. Is it shrill? Is it loud and threatening?

PUTTING PRIDE ASIDE

No, it is not easy. As you grow into adulthood and become more independent you are expected to act differently from the way you did as a child. You may still hold many of the same feelings, but the way you express those feeling is expected to change. However, you cannot expect to act totally different overnight. Developing a new, adult image takes time and lots of adjustment. To start, you may have to be the first to come forward and apologize, even though you feel you are not to blame. You may have to put your pride aside and ask for forgiveness.

As difficult as it may be for you to do these things, realize also that it may not work the first time. You may be met with a cold stare, or silence, or even an insult. You may be yelled at or laughed at. But the relationship is worth saving. A second or even a third attempt may be in order.

Do not waste weeks or months brooding or not speaking to your sibling for something that was said to you in anger. Those months may turn to years, and before you realize it a whole lifetime may pass before amends are made. Some times it becomes too late, when a sibling dies. Then the sorrow and guilt are carried long after.

The following is a letter that was written to Ann Landers by a sister who learned the value of reconciling a relationship before it was too late*:

My sister and I did not speak for twenty years. I tried once to patch things up, but she was stubborn and refused to meet me halfway. I was too proud to try again...until Mother's Day. I began to think about Mom and how sad this rift would have made her. I decided to swallow my pride and try one last time.

To my surprise, my sister was thrilled to hear my voice. We had so much catching up to do, so much to tell one another. All the bad times were forgotten, and we both felt as if we had never been apart.

Ann, we are in our seventies now. What a waste of twenty years. We could have shared so many wonderful times. I have read your words so often, "forgive and forget." I'm ashamed that it took me so long to take your advice.

I hope that my letter will encourage others who are hanging on to old grievances to learn from my experience. I haven't felt so lighthearted in years.

So thank you, Ann, for what you have done for our entire family. For the first time in years I feel whole. And my sister says she feels the same way. Keep this

Anonymous Please

If you are presently involved in a sibling conflict, decide that you are going to make the effort. Open the door to peace, even if it means that you are the one to come

---

* *Ann Landers*, Chicago Daily News, *Los Angeles Times Syndicate*.

forward first. Let go of the hostility, the suspicion, the mistrust, the resentment. Strive for a sibling relationship that is based on trust and friendship. It's worth it!

CHAPTER 2

Birth Order

"Star light, star bright, first star I see tonight, I wish I may, I wish I might, Have the wish I wish tonight...a baby sister!"

Janice remembers clearly that wish she made one summer night about eleven years ago. She also remembers making the same request from Santa at Christmas and again over the candles of her birthday cake.

One day, to her surprise and delight, she was granted her wish. Megan was born, and Janice vividly recalls the day her mother brought the baby home from the hospital. Megan was placed gently in Janice's lap, and Janice thought she looked like an angel. She had a round, pink face and beautiful dark eyelashes. Megan's tiny hand gripped Janice's finger and held on tightly.

Cute little Megan. Everyone came to see her. Everyone loved to hold her, to sing to her, and to make her smile. They ooohed and aaahed and laughed when she made funny faces. But as the years went by everyone continued to treat Megan the same way. Janice could not understand what all the fuss was about. Megan was eight and they still delighted in her every move. Janice sang and made funny faces but nobody seemed to notice.

Even now, at ten, Megan is still considered the baby of the family. Janice is the one who baby-sits for Megan on the evenings when their parents go out. Janice braids Megan's hair for her and often helps with her homework and school projects.

Janice, as always, is her mother's helper, running to get this, running to get that, even though Megan is old enough to help and often is in the very same room.

Janice feels that it will always be this way, even when they are adults and out on their own. She can't imagine Megan actually thinking or doing things on her own without someone looking out for her in the background. Megan will always be a follower, she feels, someone who will always enjoy attention and being taken care of.

It is interesting to note that part of what Janice perceives about the future may actually be true. Although not *all* last-born children have these tendencies, studies have shown that a majority do continue into adult life with the same characteristics they had when growing up.

Firstborn children like Janice are often the ones who are picked to do the errands. They tend to grow up faster and are known to be well organized and achievers. They learn to initiate activities and follow through on matters.

Just as astrologers predict what personalities fit each birth sign, so too psychologists predict what traits birth order plays in individual development.

*   *   *

Study the chart and see if you agree with its findings.

FIRSTBORN	High achiever	Well organized
	Generally on time	Rule abiding
	Reliable	Leader
MIDDLE CHILD	Has many friends	Peacemaker
	Avoids conflict	Sometimes feels unloved
	Learns to give and take	Loyal
YOUNGEST CHILD	Loves the limelight	Blames others
	Often called by nickname	People person
	Show-off	Most pampered
ONLY CHILD	Articulate	Somewhat self-centered
	Mature	Well-mannered
	Shy in group	Critical of self
TWINS	Competitive	Have one best friend
	Need to be noticed	Feel special

THE NEED TO BE NOTICED

Each of us has struggled for our place in the family at one time or another. Whether it is a struggle to be heard or seen, or to be understood, we are asking someone else to look away from all the others and see *us*. To recognize *us* for the moment and to give *us* a singular pat on the back. In larger families with many to compete with, this may be a more difficult task. In small families with no competition, it is much easier.

In a traditional family it is often true that the oldest gets the most responsibility and the youngest is the last one asked to do something. In modern families children are brought up by all kinds of people: aunts, cousins, governesses. It is really the relationship among you that is important, not the title.

Many family relationships never change. The baby of the family always remains the baby, even though he may be seventy-five-year-old Elmer John with fifteen great grandchildren.

A middle child in a large group of siblings often grows up to be happy and energetic, surrounded by friends and acquaintances (a remembrance of how it was growing up in the family). In all likelihood it is this middle child who plans the family reunions, who plays ball at the picnics, who joins the football game on Sunday afternoons.

We can't help the way we act or feel about the world as adults. It has been that way from birth. Our traits are instilled in us from the day we are born. If we were the firstborn to adoring parents, our first steps were greeted with excitement and enthusiasm. Our first words were applauded and recorded. It was a good feeling to be recognized and appreciated, and as we grew older we held on to many of those feelings. We learned to enjoy praise for accomplishments in school and later in work. And so the reliable, studious achievers are born and molded into persons who still enjoy the attention of a job well done.

ONLIES

Are you or do you know someone who is an only child? How does that compare with someone who is the number two child among six? Sometimes the differences are not readily seen but on closer examination can be discerned.

Birth statistics show that only children are unique. They are often mature children who grow into mature adults. They may be labeled "little adults" by their parents. Only children do not have to worry about sharing with brothers and sisters. They do not have fights over privacy or have to take turns doing things such as watching TV or playing a record on the stereo.

Many only children are happy with the way things

turned out in their family. They like not having to vie for attention from their parents. They like the special feeling of being the one and only and resent it when others ask if they feel they are missing something not having brothers and sisters around.

Other only children say that they wish things were different. They feel that they *are* missing out on valuable sibling relationships. Many say that they themselves will have lots of children to compensate for what they feel they have missed.

The way parents feel about having an only child plays a major role in how the child feels about it. If the parents planned on having only one child, there is less of a problem. They don't wish for more children, they enjoy the one they have. But if parents of an only child wish for more children and can't have them, or talk about feelings of regret, those feelings are transferred to the child. The child gets the feeling that somehow the family is incomplete.

If you are not an only child, perhaps you know someone who is. Is this person somewhat shy? Does the person seem uncomfortable in a group?

Next time you want to label a person as introverted, find out if he or she happens to be an only child. If so, realize where those tendencies may be coming from. The person may not have been exposed to many of the outside influences and activities that others have. He or she may not have had to withstand the daily bickering over space and belongings that kids in large families do.

Only children may appear quiet in groups of people because they are not used to having to mediate or voice differences of opinion. Although only children often complain of being lonely and isolated, many look back and see their earlier years as a most rewarding, fulfilling, and creative period. They enjoyed being the "main attraction" in their parents' lives and say that, given the choice, they would not have had it any other way.

MIDDLE CHILDREN

It is surprising to hear experts say that middle children have the fewest pictures in the family album, but studies prove it to be true. Think about it. Maybe it is not so extraordinary.

We all know that the firstborn's entrance into this world is probably the most exciting thing that has occurred in a parent's life. The firstborn has snapshots taken while still in the womb. Then after the birth come pictures of first cries, first teeth, first haircuts.

The last-born child has pictures up on the mantel long after the other children have left home. But somehow the middle children do get lost in the shuffle. They have the usual birthday pictures pasted in the album, but many of their achievements are forgotten in the commotion.

Middle children quickly learn to give and take. As adults they have many friends around them, taking the place of brothers and sisters. They are loyal, but sometimes they feel unloved.

Dr. Kevin Leman, in *The Birth Order Book*, talks about the middle child: "...if any generalizations can be made about the middle child, it is that they feel squeezed and/or dominated. It is important for parents to be extra aware that the middle child often feels as if 'everybody is running my life.' Not only does the middle child have a set of parents in authority over him, but he has an older sibling right there also."

Middle children may indeed get the hand-me-downs and feel overlooked, but they learn early how to get out of sticky situations. How easy it is to have older brother Billy to blame for a misdeed, or three-year-old Ellen.

One common complaint among middle children is that they feel overlooked by their parents and overshadowed by their siblings. If they have something exciting or interesting to tell their parents, the parents may be engrossed in another child's problems at the time. They have to wait for the right time or the right place to speak, and often their problems fall on deaf or distracted ears.

Middle children appreciate the closeness of a big family at holiday time and during crises. Many agree that it is nice having someone close who will always understand you. "I like being number three brother of six," says one sophomore. "It's like being in camp...there's always someone to talk to, anytime, day or night."

ROCKABYE

Once the baby, always the baby, the expression goes. Ninety-six-year-old William Sommers is still Little Billy to the Sommers family. His eighty-nine-year-old sister Margaret still fixes his hot chocolate with two marshmallows just as she did when they were children.

Cute, somewhat immature, charming, and basking in attention are some of the characteristics attributed to last-born children.

"You'll always be my baby," says the fifty-five-year-old mother to her thirty-year-old three-hundred-pound linebacker for the Greenbay Packers.

The baby of the family is the one who is worried about the most. Is he warm? Is he happy? Is he safe? The others may be on their own—but I still have my Thomas. Sound familiar?

Last-born children are often coddled long after they are

out of the house and living on their own. They continue to enjoy the limelight, even as adults, and are known to be "people pleasers."

Last-born children tend to get the blame from others in the family. They often have a hard time getting themselves out of sticky situations. After all, whom else can they pass the blame to down the line? Although older brothers and sisters often use the youngest as a scapegoat, they also are protective of him or her in the outside world. It is the older ones who look after their younger siblings, especially in school situations. If the youngest is being picked on by bullies, the older ones come to the rescue. One forty-year-old father of four told me that he still protects his younger sister. If problems arise within the family he tries to solve everything himself, because he does not want his sister to have to be involved or to worry.

DOUBLE TROUBLE

Every birth order has inherent strengths and weaknesses. Even twins. As many twins admit, having or being a twin is not always a wonderful thing. Twins share special problems not known to other brothers and sisters.

- Twins feel that they are regarded as a unit, a *we* instead of an *I*.
- Twins often grow up competitive.
- Twins are often overlooked for singular accomplishments.
- Twins sometimes feel different, especially when people stare or ask questions about how it feels to be a twin.

The main feeling that twins share is closeness, something that starts at birth. It is true that twins are looked upon with awe by many. They mirror each other's actions and often watch each other's every move.

What is nice about this special closeness is that twins seldom feel lonely in childhood. They always have someone to play with, someone the same age to talk to and confide in.

As the mother of boy/girl twins (age eight) I myself find it comforting, because I know that my twins will never lack companionship. They get in fights with children at school over the usual things, but they always have someone with whom to discuss their problems, someone their exact age who will listen and understand.

I have read in many books about twins that they have a special bond, and now I believe that it is true. If one of my twins is hurting, either physically or emotionally, the other is close by, sometimes even voicing the same complaint. I remember when the twins were three and my daughter had a bad flu virus. She woke up at night coughing. I went to give her cough medicine but was taken aback by what I saw. Her brother was standing at her bedside trying to give her a drink of water and patting her back. The scene was touching, and I know that special closeness they feel will always be with them.

The source of competitiveness in twins is great also. While both strive for parental attention in the earlier years, the competition often lasts in the adult years as well.

Because twins are looked upon as being different, they are often popular with their classmates and attract many friends. They may be referred to as "the twins" rather than by name. Studies have shown that twins remain close long after childhood and often throughout their lives.

As you can see, our birth order does have a direct effect on how we relate to our brothers and sisters. Do you feel that you are still treated like a baby by an older sibling?

Perhaps you are the oldest and feel weighed down with responsibility. The following are first-person contributions by students who have expressed their thoughts and feelings on the subject of birth order.

"My older brothers have moved out of the house. Mom and Dad always seem depressed. They talk about how they miss Josh and Terry and how quiet the place is without them. It makes me feel like I don't count. The fact that I am here doesn't mean as much in my parents' eyes."

Stuart, 14

"I'm the youngest. What makes me angry is that I'm always left out of family business. My vote never counts. They never ask me about my choices in decisions that will affect all of us."

Rita, 16

"Being the youngest of twelve children presented some problems. I felt I had several mothers and fathers. I always felt that they did not take me seriously, and I had a severe need to contribute to the family but was not able to. To some extent, I became self-centered and self-devoted. There was a twenty-year-span from the oldest to the youngest."

Rose, 48

"I'm in the middle and I love it. If Mom is after us for something that one of us did, I can always weasel out of it. I have learned how to pass things off to the older and younger ones. Middle children get away with more."

Tracy, 16

"I'm the oldest in my family. It's only me and my little

brother. There are eight years between us. He's seven and I'm fifteen. I feel that I am 'breaking in' my parents in everything, from curfew to boyfriend problems. Since I'm a girl, my parents tend to worry more about me than my brother, but he will not be able to get away with the things I do because they will already know. I get good grades, but I do have the pressure of always making my parents proud of me."

Natasha, 15

"I am ten and have a twin brother and sister who are seven. We always fight. I feel that the twins get more attention. Sometimes I feel left out. I want to be included but they are close. My parents give me special attention for certain things, like good grades. It makes me sad when I fight with the twins because they keep coming back at me, so I fight it out and we settle it. If I had my choice, I'd like to be a middle child because you can have special relationships with younger and older brothers and sisters."

Barry, 10

"As an only child I believe it took me longer to grow up and accept responsibility. I never had to do much, because my parents saw to it that I had everything I wanted. I was like their main project. When they both came home from work they talked to me about what happened in their day. They asked me about mine.

If I really wanted something, I didn't have to wait long to get it. Some people may think that I am spoiled, but I know my parents acted that way for a reason. Mom was told that she couldn't have children. Their adoption papers were already being processed when she became pregnant with me. They were excited, to say the least.

Sometimes I mind being an only child, but I like not having to share my things with anyone else. It is quiet in my house, and when we visit my aunt and uncle and four cousins it is crazy over there. I kind of enjoy the noise."

Ramon, 19

"I am the oldest. Being the oldest girl in a family of girls is not easy. My father treats me like the boy he never had and expects me to excel in everything I do. While there are special privileges, like being chosen by my mother to stay up and watch the late movie with her, there are a lot more stresses. Being the oldest, you feel a lot of guilt about family problems because you are old enough for your parents to let you in on things.

Chantell, 16

"Up until recently there wasn't a whole lot to be proud of in my siblings. They were born in the '50s and adolescents in the late '60s and early '70s, and by the early '80s they were all recovering from some sort of long-term substance abuse. I am proud of their strength, which has brought them out of it. I am especially proud of their respective achievements since recovering.

I think if anything they were envious of my ability to communicate with our parents and tolerate our parents' struggles. I know my sisters were jealous of the attention that I received, but my attitude is that if you are not willing to compromise occasionally, you probably don't deserve their attention and support."

Cory, 18

"I sometimes feel that my older sister has more than

me. I'm just starting college because I have been working at a dull job that I'm not thrilled with. She has a job that she likes. I do not have what she has so I feel that I am not that happy with my life. I try not to compare myself with her but Mom always says, 'Why aren't you as happy as your sister?' She always compares us, and that makes me mad."

Kyla, 19

"I love my younger brother. We get along quite well. I feel sorry for him because he gets yelled at a lot. My friends are very outgoing and adventurous, so I do more and go out more than my brother. I feel that I have accomplished more, but maybe he'll do the same by the time he is my age."

Miriam, 15

KNOWLEDGE MAKES THE DIFFERENCE

Growing up is not easy for anyone. With the jealousy and anger that can prevail between brothers and sisters, it is a wonder that siblings don't kill each other. Many arguments get to the edge of disaster but somehow are pulled back and defused before anything really terrible happens.

Your order of birth plays a major role in how you react to these types of situations. If you are the oldest, fighting with a younger sibling, you may have a tendency to be impatient. You may brush off what a brother is trying to convey to you and merely pacify him. That, in turn, makes him angry and frustrated, and he does things deliberately to get back at you.

Following are *action steps* that can help you deal with sibling conflicts:

- If you are the youngest and feel that you are constantly left out of family decisions, *speak up*. Explain to your parents and older siblings that you want to be included. You are part of the family too! No one sibling should always dominate.

- Are you the oldest child with all the responsibility? *Delegate* smaller tasks for younger brothers and sisters. Engage their cooperation. *Ask* for their help first, then gradually let them take on some of your overload. Show your parents that your younger brothers or sisters are capable of doing the tasks.

- Do you feel caught in the middle? *Take part* in the family's admiration of other siblings' accomplishments but work at achieving your own. Discuss with your parents your need for private time with them. Plan an afternoon or evening with them away from the rest.

- Are you a lonely only? When and if you feel the need for companionship other than parents, *invite friends* to your home. Have small parties or get-togethers. Join after-school activities. If you have cousins your age, attend family functions. Invite cousins to spend time at your home.

- Twins do not have to dress alike. Work at *developing your own friends*. Have individuals values, likes and dislikes. Value your closeness with your twin, but do not go along with his or her way of thinking if it is different from your own. Learn to act independently. Do not be afraid that if separated, your twin might not make it or might get into serious trouble without you.

IDENTIFYING CONFLICT

Experts agree that sibling problems, real or imagined, are a major part of conflict in the family. But how can one tell the difference between a real and an imagined problem?

I spoke with three groups of teens at a local high school and asked them to assist me in a project. Each was to write down the major source of conflict in their relationship with a sibling. Then each was to ask the sibling to write down what he or she felt was the main source of irritation in the relationship. Many students were quick to answer: phone privileges; bad attitudes; invasion of privacy.

The results were most interesting, especially to the students themselves. Sixteen-year-old Scott insisted that the main beef between himself and his brother Sam involved the use of the phone. He complained that Sam had a habit of tying up the phone after school and on weekends. They fought bitterly over this, and Scott was certain that Sam would agree.

Scott went home and asked his brother to write down what he thought was the worst conflict between them. What Sam wrote down was something that Scott hardly considered a problem: He was angriest with Scott when Scott played his stereo loud on Sunday morning, the only morning that Sam could sleep late. The rock music began at eight in the morning, and even though the boys had separate rooms, the noise traveled through the wall and into Sam's room, waking him up.

Scott laughed when he heard what Sam considered major. When he told Sam about the phone issue, Sam was surprised. I asked Scott if it would bother him much to curtail his Sunday morning stereo playing until his brother was up and out of the house. Scott agreed and a few days later said that Sam had agreed to share the phone time.

The boys worked out their differences by getting them into perspective first, then compromising, a give-and-take situation.

Below are the answers of some students and the corresponding answers of their siblings. It is interesting to see how differently most of them view the areas of conflict.

MAJOR ISSUE	MAJOR ISSUE
Brad, 15, is angriest when his sister's friends are allowed in his room when he is away and use his video and computer equipment.	Jerilyn, 12, says Brad does not admit leaving things around the house. Their mother makes her clean up Brad's mess and she gets blamed for his sloppiness.
Shelley 18, is livid when her sister Molly takes the family car without asking. Shelley is often left without transportation to her afternoon job.	Molly, 17, hates it when Shelley wears Molly's clothes without permission.
Randi, 16, gets most upset with her twin sister Robyn because she feels that Robyn flirts with her boyfriend.	Robyn, 16, admits that this is their main source of conflict but disagrees with her sister's accusations. She says that she is just acting friendly and that Randi is scared of losing her boyfriend to anyone because she is so insecure.
Adam, 19, has the worst fights with his two brothers when they borrow his music cassette tapes and don't return them. He sometimes finds that they have lent his tapes to their friends.	Chris, 16, and Jeff, 14, say that their major complaint is that Adam bullies them. They say that Adam is bigger and stronger and uses his size to push them around, especially when their parents are not present.
Melanie, 17, is angriest when	Michael, 12, agrees that he often

MAJOR ISSUE	*MAJOR ISSUE*
Michael reads her diary when she is not around.	sneaks a look at his sister's diary, but he says that his major complaint is that she sulks when she doesn't get her own way.

As you can see, each person has an individual idea of where the sibling conflict lies. When this difference of opinion occurs, it may actually make the problems easier to resolve. What you thought of as an important obstacle in your relationship may in fact be just a minor inconvenience to your sibling. It is something that can be worked out. The process involves give and take and asking questions.

- Do you really get angry when I play my music on Sunday mornings? Okay, I'll switch days if you'll...
- Do you really think I flirt with your boyfriend? I'm not doing it intentionally, but I'll try to watch myself in the future, if you'll promise to...
- I realize that I sulk a lot. I didn't think you noticed or that it was that big a deal with you. I'll try not to do it if you will stop...

Give and take. It works in all kinds of relationships, at home, in school, and in the workforce. Next time you find yourself grumbling about something your sibling has done, come forward and ask him or her if he realizes how it bothers you. Explain your feelings. Then ask what about you bothers him or her. The conversation is open for discussion between you. Promise to pull back on what makes your sibling angry and ask him or her to do likewise.

Give and take, action steps, and a better understanding of the problems are the ingredients for a better relationship between you in the future.

BE OPEN TO CHANGE

During these adolescent years, your sibling relationships will go through changes. These changes can occur in many ways. Each of you grows and develops and may have a change of attitude toward the other.

Sometimes the older brother or sister leaps ahead in maturity, and the source of conflict becomes different. Older siblings may become like parents to younger ones. Whereas the younger ones were once considered a major headache, the older ones now have more patience and tolerance with them, and the younger ones look to the older siblings for guidance. Once troubled relationships can develop into rewarding ones.

Dr. Lee Salk, a leading psychologist, in his book *Ask Dr. Salk*, had this to say about change and about growing up.

". . . life is, in a sense, a series of changes in our feelings, desires, and needs. As we pass through various stages of life, these changes can cause confusion and uncertainty, and the problems can appear insurmountable; most of this works out in time, and new feelings become more comfortable as we develop as individuals."

A LETTER FROM JOANNE

Before winding up this chapter on birth order and relationships, I would like to share with you a letter from a woman named Joanne. Joanne is the mother of two young children, and I know from talking with her in the past that she has had a most turbulent and emotional relationship with her younger sister. I asked Joanne if she would be willing to contribute her thoughts and feelings on that, and she agreed.

"I am thirty-six years old, and I have many memories of my past with my younger sister. Since I have reached this age, I have had time to look back, trying to make sense and understand what happened between my sister and myself.

I remember always loving my sister. I took care of her and protected her. She was like my first baby. I need to mention that I was born with a minor flaw (eye imperfection), and I believe that probably had a lot to do with our relationship.

I wasn't the prettiest of children and she was. Because of my affliction I learned at an early age my place, so to speak. I was always in the background, and my sister was the center of attention.

At the time I thought I liked it, but as I got older it brought me a lot of pain.

Being raised in a European household contributed to our conflicts. Because I was the oldest, I was to show the example. My sister called me the "goody-goody" (which I suppose I was), and I listened to her. She used to get into trouble for one reason or another. Our biggest jealousy was who could gain our parents' attention.

I was quiet and received my attention that way. She was louder and received hers that way.

Our teenage years were the worst of times. I feel that my sister manipulated me, and I allowed it at the time because I was unaware. I often felt hostility toward my parents and my sister.

At present, my sister and I are not speaking. For a while I thought we were on the right track. We both married. I have two children and she has one. We finally had something in common that we could share (I thought).

Time has passed, and I have realized that what I needed was to be free. I have always been there for my sister, even with the pain I felt and hurt feelings. I realize my mistakes. I was like a second mother to her, and she resented it. Maybe I stopped her from growing up.

I try to see her in a different light, but I haven't been able to let go of hurt feelings from the past. These feelings haunt me.

My feelings for my sister I know are bizarre. I'm not even sure what they are. I have them locked away, and I'm just trying to live my life. I think what I have is a love/hate feeling for her, which pains me, but I cannot find it in my heart to call her and make up. I have done that my whole life just to keep the peace, and I'm tired of doing it.

I can't say how she feels toward me today. I haven't a clue. She probably has a love/hate feeling for me as well. Sometimes I feel as though we were raised as one and I finally broke away.

I believe that many things contribute to sibling rivalry: society, what's happening at the moment, age differences, how parents treat each child, and what parents expect of their children.

Having my own children is not easy. I have learned that each child has its own special quality and has its own special needs; therefore they should be dealt with individually and not the same.

Joanne

It is important to realize that as you grow older relationships change. Some siblings grow apart, and many who were not close are drawn together. It is during this time that brothers and sisters begin to reexamine their relationships. Petty disagreements are overlooked, and amends are made for past differences. You begin to see things differently and appreciate each other more.

Later, when you have families of your own, the close or renewed relationship with your sibling prevails because you share many memories. Most of the funny, happy, ridiculous moments you will remember are the ones you are experiencing right now. The fighting and making up, the embarrassing things that are said or done are memories in the making. Soon you will be asking each other—Do you remember when Mom and Dad did this? How about the time our sister did that and we—

Siblings have always struggled for their place in the family and always will, but it can be useful and constructive for both parents and children because it involves competition. Competing helps us to measure and improve our abilities. It is a fair and honest challenge.

We all derive satisfaction from personal achievement and recognition and want our parents and the world to know that we are somebody. When we were younger and growing up in a busy household, we were saying to our parents: I count—Don't talk over me, around me—Don't laugh at my opinions—Don't ignore me, shut me out— There may be others older or younger than I in this house, but I want to be seen and heard.

Where you stand in the family line-up does indeed have an effect on how you relate to siblings and to others. But try to remember these important points:

- Be on the lookout for failures in communication.
- Be willing to compromise or change.
- It's never too late to renew a sibling relationship that has gone wrong.

- Stand up and voice your opinion if you feel you are being overlooked.

The sibling relationship can be a challenging and meaningful source of interaction. Each family strength builds upon another. How you feel or what you say is an important contribution.

As we know, struggles with brothers and sisters do not end with the end of adolescence. They continues long after. However, solid family bonds created now can be a great source of joy throughout adult life.

CHAPTER 3

Stepsiblings

Danny knew it was going to be a bad day because of the way it started out. He was shaken out of a deep sleep at 5:00 a.m. by his mother. It was raining, and the room was dark and cold. Today was the day he was going to live with his new stepdad and stepbrother, Kevin.

His mother would be driving them the 150 miles to a small town where they would begin their life together as a new family. Danny was nervous. He had met Kevin only three times before, twice at family dinners and one weekend during Thanksgiving. Kevin was a year older, and it had been decided that the boys would share a room.

Danny thought it was unfair that it was he who had to be uprooted from his friends and his school. He was happy where he was and didn't want anything to change. But his mother and Kevin's father, Bob, had married last weekend after six months of dating, and suddenly he found himself saying good-bye to people and places that he had known all his life.

His bags were packed. Deciding to skip breakfast,

he loaded the things his mother had packed into the van. Many things were running through Danny's mind. What would it be like sharing a room with someone he hardly knew? Would Bob treat the two boys equally, or would he show favoritism toward Kevin? And what about friends? Would Kevin introduce him to his friends, or would he have to make it on his own socially?

The fact that no one had consulted him about these arrangements made it frustrating for Danny. He knew that even if he put up a fuss about the situation it would not help in the least. His mother was happy and in love. Everything would work out for them, just give it a chance, she told him.

As it turned out, it *was* tough for Danny. Many of the problems he predicted came about just as he had expected. But it was also tough for Kevin. He was apprehensive too. There were new house rules to abide by and many compromises that had to be worked out. The boys fought bitterly over territory; where their beds would be positioned, on which side of the room their personal belongings would be put, on whose dresser the radio would be placed. Kevin did not like having to share his room. He felt an immediate lack of privacy.

Feelings of jealousy also arose between the boys. Each tried to outdo the other in efforts to win their parents' favor and attention. Sometimes they even got in trouble deliberately so that their parents would pay special attention to them for their wrongdoing. Both were trying to establish themselves in the new family unit and using whatever means it took to accomplish it.

It did not come about overnight. It did not even come about easily. But after almost a year of having to adjust,

Danny's new family began to feel like the real thing. He felt that he had a home where he was loved and respected, and he in turn began to give of himself to his family.

That is how it happens in many blended families that are formed after the death of a parent or a divorce. Two people decide to marry, and an instant family is created. Stepsiblings are thrown together and expected to act like brothers and sisters immediately. In reality, it is not that simple. Many areas have to be worked out. Many feelings have to be acknowledged and expressed.

Picture yourself going to visit a cousin or a friend in another state. It's fun and exciting. You both have so much to catch up on from your last stay. You share a room and stay up talking until the late hours. Then before you know it it is time to go home. You promise to write, give your hugs, and return to your own home and your own family.

Imagine for a moment that just as you were about to leave you were told that you were not going anywhere. This would be your home from now on. You and your cousin or friend would be bunking together permanently. Your family situation had changed, and things were going to be different from now on. But don't worry, everything will turn out all right for you.

You do worry. You worry about how it will be living in your new environment, meeting your new stepsibling's friends, getting along with your new family, and many other things. You want to go back where you felt safe and sure. You want things to be as they used to be, but no one is asking for your opinion. They are telling you what you will be doing and whom you will be living with, and you are supposed to be happy and calm about the change in your life.

Just as it took Danny and Kevin months before they felt comfortable with each other, so it is with many stepsiblings. So many areas have to be worked out between stepsiblings, but one important feeling often surfaces: suspicion.

- Is she being nice to me because she married my dad and wants to show him that she is a good mother, or does she really like me for myself?
- Do my stepsiblings accept me because they feel sorry for me, or am I really a part of their family as they say I am?
- Did Dad marry her because he loves her or because he feels we need a mother to raise us?
- Does my stepbrother really want me hanging out with his friends as he says, or does he feel bad because I haven't met anyone since I came to live with my new stepfamily?

It can be frustrating. Besides suspicion, other problems arise: new dinner hours, changes in curfews, adjustment of TV and phone privileges. Some things have to be settled, such as who does what jobs, and who has the right to tell someone else what to do.

Parents have to set guidelines that will affect everyone in the household. You may have been allowed to stay out until midnight on weekends when you were living alone with your dad, but your stepmom has other ideas. Her rule is 10:30, and you are expected to abide by it.

You are angry and feel that she is being unfair. But these are some of the changes that you have to expect and get used to. Realize that your parents are in charge of house rules and that they expect and need your cooperation.

CONTRACTS

In addition to abiding by new parental rules, there is also the difficult task of settling differences between you and your stepsiblings. For the first time in your life you may be having to share, to compromise, to adapt to value systems that are different from your own.

When there is a vast area of difference between you and your stepsiblings and conflict arises daily, it might help to sit down and draw up a contract between you. Talk openly about what is fair. Ask what will work for them and explain what will work for you. You may want to set down a list of rules that are agreeable to all of you. For example:

- No borrowing clothes without asking first.
- Stereo off by 9:00 on school nights.
- All phone messages posted on the board.

An actor signs a contract with a production company to do something (act) in return for compensation and publicity. A home buyer signs a contract with a real estate company for the purchase of a house. A borrower signs a contract for the loan of money. The parties agree, and if the contract is broken the one who breaks it must pay the price.

A contract can be drawn for any purpose as long as it is agreed upon by the involved parties. If you and your stepsiblings decide to devise a contract between you, here are some points to remember when writing it up:

- Be clear and specific.
- Define what is important.
- Agree on what is fair.
- Allow for exceptions.

Decide what the consequences will be for the one who

does not abide by the rules. The person who breaks the contract should have to pay a penalty.

Stepsiblings Peter and Donna devised such a contract. Although Donna was fourteen and Peter eighteen, they realized that many areas had to be worked out between them now that they were living together as brother and sister. They lived in a small high-rise apartment with their parents. A big issue was whose turn it was each weekend morning to get up early and take the dog out. Both liked to sleep late on Saturday and Sunday mornings, and a fight was brewing in the family over the issue. The two negotiated a verbal contract: Donna would get up early on Saturdays, letting Peter sleep late, and Peter would take Sunday mornings. It worked. Of course, there were exceptions, but they had allowed for that in the initial agreement. On one Saturday Peter had early football practice and a late party. He asked Donna to change days so that he could sleep in on Sunday morning, and Donna agreed.

Each contract should be written or discussed, spelling out what is fair and which people are involved. Below are some examples of contracts between stepsiblings.

Robin	Jan	Arturo	Ken	Cheryl
Help Arturo on his paper route. Pack Jan's lunch in the mornings.	Feed Arturo's gerbil. Start the coffee in the morning for Robin and Arturo. Take Robin's phone messages.	Help Robin with algebra. Drive Jan and friends to mall on Sunday afternoons. Take Robin to lunch if she helps on paper route.	Cheryl cannot borrow tapes without permission. Gets to choose TV programs Monday and Wednesday nights. Dries dishes.	Gets to use the bathroom first in the morning. Chooses TV programs Tuesday and Friday nights. Washes dinner dishes.

GETTING TO KNOW EACH OTHER

Having a brother or sister suddenly appear in your life can be an emotional experience. You may feel totally helpless because for the most part the decision was not yours to make. At first you may feel shy and want to withdraw from everyone. After looking your new stepsiblings over you may decide that you don't want them for your brothers and sisters. When you realize that you have little choice in the decision, you feel angry and may take that anger out on your parent.

Try to understand that these feelings are normal. Stepsiblings have felt everything from hatred and rage to violence after being told that they would be uniting with a new family. One person said that he threatened to kill himself if his father went through with the marriage and forced him to live with four kids whom he hated. Of course, he didn't carry out his threat, but his anger was so deep that the family were in counseling for two years before they were able to live comfortably with each other.

While there are many such stories of stepsibling relationships, so are there successes and happy stories. Many teens have found exciting new relationships in their stepfamilies. They love and care about their stepsiblings as if they were blood-related. The vast variety of feelings shows that the blending of two families is emotional. First impressions are not lasting impressions. In fact, they may be just a cover-up of feelings.

If your stepsibling seems cold and unloving, there may be another reason for his or her actions. The coldness or indifference may be from fear that you will take away the parent's love. It is difficult enough to have to share a personal item with a stepsibling, or a room, or a friend. But a parent? That may be the ultimate fear and concern of the child. To have to allow someone else into your life to share your parent's love and attention is scary. You may ask, will there be enough left for me? What if Mom or Dad end up liking my stepsibling more than me?

STEPPARENTS

Stepparents themselves play a major role in their children's feelings of confusion and insecurity. First, stepparents are very conscious of what is going on when they bring the two families together. They too are nervous about the outcome. Most come from emotional breaks with past partners, either through death or divorce. Their worries are much like their children's worries—about acceptance and about fitting in.

Stepmothers especially want to be sure they are saying or doing the right thing. They want to be accepted by their new children and dispel the myth of the evil stepmother in such stories as "Cinderella."

Many stepparents believe that they are being watched and judged by others, such as teachers, grandparents, cousins, and neighbors. Sometimes they find themselves trying too hard to be a good parent. They want so much to do a good job that it becomes a serious endeavor. They tread lightly and try to justify words and actions when they should be just acting naturally. Stepmothers wonder: Was I fair? Did I yell too loudly? Were they dressed appropriately for church? Just as adoptive parents feel a bit of unsureness and excitement when their baby is first brought to them, so too do stepparents.

Seymour Reit in his book *Sibling Rivalry* says, "The inner tug-of-war puts an extra burden on a stepparent in handling sibling rivalry and similar problems. It's harder for a stepfather, for example, to break up a fight between his own child and a stepchild without risking favoritism, and deep down this adult may indeed question his own motives."

Barbara is stepmother to three children, eight, four, and two. She is having difficulty in her new role because of something that she is embarrassed to talk freely about. Her eight-year-old stepdaughter Tina reminds her of her new husband's ex-wife Jeannette. The girl is the image of her mother, from her curly red hair to her slow, easy manner of speaking. There was a messy divorce between the two couples, and harsh words went back and forth between Jeannette and Barbara.

Things have since calmed down, and Jeannette has remarried and moved to another town. But Barbara is raising Jeannette's daughter and is reminded of her every day. Barbara finds herself trying extra hard to love and be patient with Tina and feels guilty about her feelings toward her. She even admits feeling a twinge of jealousy when her husband pays extra attention to Tina. It almost seems as though Jeannette were still living with them, a reminder of the past.

Barbara's feelings are common in stepfamilies. Children are replicas of their parents. They have a blood bond. A stepchild is often a real, live reminder of the spouse's previous marriage. Stepparents find this a difficult area of adjustment.

FAILURE OF COMMUNICATION

"She treats her kids better than me!" That was Matthew's major complaint when I asked him how it felt to be a stepson and have stepsiblings. "If a choice has to be made, her kids get to choose. If her son is late coming in on a school night, he gets reprimanded. If I am late on a school night, I get grounded. I notice it all the time. Her daughter gets the last piece of pizza. If papers are scattered around the room, who has to clean them up? I do. My stepmom Rita makes it evident that I come last after her kids. It makes me angry. I know there is nothing I can do or say to top her kids. Lately I've stopped trying to compete. I hardly speak to any of them. It's obvious where I stand, so what's the use of trying anyway?"

Matthew's feelings are common. Often a stepchild feels that because he or she is not blood-related, her or his place in the family is below that of a biological child. Parents may not realize that they are acting in ways that provoke these feelings in their children.

I asked Matthew if he had ever explained his feelings to his stepmother. He said that he had never considered mentioning it because he was embarrassed. He felt that she would laugh and probably tell her kids. Then his life would surely be unbearable.

"But what have you got to lose?" I asked him. "You are only fourteen and have many more years left at home. Do you really want to continue not speaking and sulking over something that your mom may not even be aware of? She may be the one to be embarrassed, not you."

Of course, the reason behind Matthew's reluctance to reveal his feelings was that he was afraid his stepfamily would ridicule and reject him. But he agreed at least to approach his stepmother and tell her how he felt about being last.

He came back and said that he had been surprised by her response. At first Rita became defensive, and Matthew said he almost turned and walked out. But then she broke down and started to cry, telling Matthew that she was relieved he had come to her about the problem. She thought Matthew hated her, and she felt she was not doing her job as a mother. Matthew explained his feelings of favoritism in the family, and Rita understood. But she told another side of the story, one of which Matthew was not aware.

Rita explained that she was trying too hard to be a good mother to her own children because her ex-husband was in the backround always threatening to take them away from her. She was always consciously trying to say and do the right thing to prove to the kids that she was a good mother and that they should stay with her.

Rita and Matthew cleared the air by communicating their feelings. Matthew later admitted that the anger and silence on his part could have continued indefinitely and even lasted into his adult years had Rita not been made aware of her actions.

Perhaps you are feeling anger and resentment over things that are happening with your stepparents and stepsiblings but are afraid to bring them out in the open. Try to realize that they may not even be aware of your feelings unless you tell them. Your stepsister may not think twice about the fact that she shares secrets only with her biological sister. Of course you feel lonely and left out when it happens, but *she* may not know that. You will probably feel stupid and embarrassed in admitting your feelings, but after they are out in the open you will get a response. Your stepsisters will answer many of your questions, and sometimes they might not be the responses you want to hear. *They* may be angry at you and ask why you have been behaving in a certain way. But the lines of communication have been opened and perhaps the differences can be better defined and worked out on both sides.

OLD VS. NEW ATTITUDES

A new magazine is out that has a monthly column about attitudes called "Swap the Old for the New." Readers send in quotes from celebrities, and the editors place the quotes under one of two columns, Old Ways of Thinking or Modern Ways of Thinking. The magazine deals mostly with views on the feminist movement, but for the most part it does portray old and new attitudes that people are holding.

Its headline proclaims, A NEW WOMAN IS AN ATTITUDE, NOT AN AGE, but that could easily be changed to: A NEW PERSON IS AN ATTITUDE, NOT AN AGE. Past attitudes can be changed into new, meaningful ones. If we find ourselves sticking to old ways of thinking and the results are not favorable time after time, maybe it is time to change.

Katie is a professional dancer who has been appearing in Broadway musicals for the past twenty years. She has always been chosen on a first or second audition, but one time she was taken aback at what was offered her. She was asked by the director of a rock and roll musical to be a member of the chorus. Katie had a good singing voice but had never given up a dance part for a part in the chorus. The director explained to Katie that he felt she was too old for the dance parts. He was hiring only eighteen- to twenty-five-year-olds, and Katie was now well into her 40s. This had been happening a lot lately, Katie realized. She was finding it more difficult to be chosen for these types of musicals even though she was still a good dancer and in top shape and form. Katie was angry with everyone. She was mad at the director because he based his decision on age and not ability. She was upset at her husband and children for suggesting that she forgo the rock musicals and try out for other productions.

But Katie would not let go of her attitude about her dancing and herself. She decided to reject the chorus offer and continue trying out for the productions she had been dancing in for years.

Katie missed an opportunity by holding on to old attitudes and old convictions, even though they were no longer working for her. She was putting obstacles in her own way by failing to open herself up to new and exciting opportunities.

The director was not saying that Katie was a bad dancer. He was saying that he believed she had additional talent as a singer, and he was giving her the chance to perform. He was also holding to his own decision that the dance team in his show would be of a certain age. Had Katie admitted that she was no longer a twenty-year-old dancer, she could have been open to change.

Swapping old attitudes for new ones means admitting certain things to ourselves, the main one being that things just aren't working for us as they did in the past. Times are changing. Many of us have to go with the flow or be left behind. Besides opportunities, changes of attitudes can help us in relationships. Dropping old feelings or thoughts about people and changing your mind about them is a switch in attitude.

An example of this is the high school reunions that so many of us attend years after graduation. At twenty- and thirty-year reunions girls and guys sit around and talk about the others as though they were still eighteen. Some may find themselves ignoring a person by whom they were intimidated back in high school. Others wait for the class clown to come up with jokes just as he used to twenty years ago. They hold on to old convictions about what people were like back then and expect them to be the same. Some of them still may be. The homecoming queen could still be the most beautiful and popular woman in the room. But it usually does not work out that way. People change over time, and we must learn to change too.

Swapping old attitudes for new ones can also work in your present-day relationships with your stepsiblings and stepparents. The bad feelings you have been holding on to can disappear if you let them go and practice new ways of thinking about a person. Here are examples of negative feelings and attitudes that have been replaced by new, positive ones.

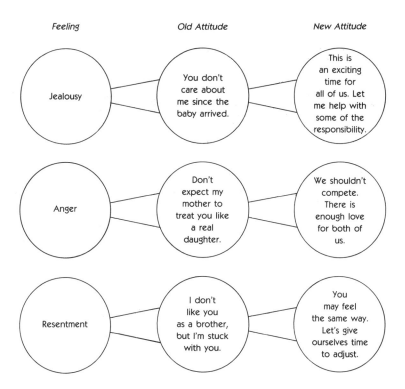

Feeling	Old Attitude	New Attitude
Jealousy	You don't care about me since the baby arrived.	This is an exciting time for all of us. Let me help with some of the responsibility.
Anger	Don't expect my mother to treat you like a real daughter.	We shouldn't compete. There is enough love for both of us.
Resentment	I don't like you as a brother, but I'm stuck with you.	You may feel the same way. Let's give ourselves time to adjust.

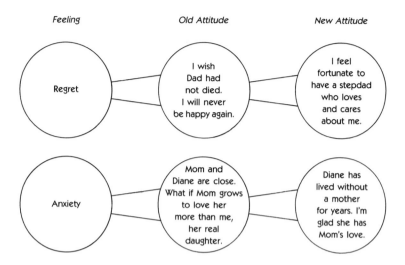

Feeling	Old Attitude	New Attitude
Regret	I wish Dad had not died. I will never be happy again.	I feel fortunate to have a stepdad who loves and cares about me.
Anxiety	Mom and Diane are close. What if Mom grows to love her more than me, her real daughter.	Diane has lived without a mother for years. I'm glad she has Mom's love.

EMMA

"My name is Emma and I am sixteen. My mother died of cancer two years ago. A few months ago my father started dating a woman named Darleen who has two kids, nine and fifteen. Her husband died in a car accident when her kids were babies.

Her fifteen-year-old daughter, Sherry, and I don't get along well at all. Sherry is loud, and she wears outrageous clothes. She wears tons of makeup and plays lead guitar in an all girl's heavy metal rock band.

I am the opposite. I guess you could say that I am on the quiet side and very conservative. Sherry acts as if I am from another planet. I know that she laughs at me behind my back, and I guess I am somewhat intimidated by her. She is the kind of girl that I go out of my way to avoid at school and at parties.

Once I tried talking with her brother, Mark, because it looks as if our parents are going to get married and I wanted to get to know him better. He was cold to me and even said that he hoped our parents didn't get married because he didn't want another father. That hurt. I was angry at everyone, at Dad, at Sherry, at Mark, and at Darleen.

I went to Dad and told him how upset I was and how I was against his marrying Darleen. I even threatened to run away and said that in the end he would have to choose between Darleen and me.

My father was hurt and angry with me for acting that way. He said that he planned to ask Darleen to marry him and that all of us kids would have to learn to adjust and to live with one another. I saw the whole mess as a no-win situation. Everyone is still angry and holding to their positions."

Emma's story is not unusual. What she is feeling is fear. She admits being angry with everyone, but her anger is a cover-up for her fear about losing her father to another woman. With her mother's death still fresh in her mind and her heart, she is just beginning to adjust to coping without her. She sees Darleen's family as a threat. Her father has been both mother and father to her, and now there is someone else wanting his love and attention. Emma is not ready to let go.

Emma's hurt and anger at her father and the whole situation were making her an emotional wreck. She finally decided to seek the advice of her school counselor. This is what happened:

Mr. Pearce, the guidance counselor, asked Emma to participate in an exercise, and she agreed. Emma was to write down on index cards all the feelings that she was experiencing about her father and the prospective step-family. When all the cards were displayed they revealed only negative thoughts and accusations toward Sherry, her father, and Darleen. The counselor then asked Emma to flip over each card and write a few positive feelings about the situation. Emma could not think of one. She sat and chewed her pencil. She began writing something but quickly scratched it out.

"Not one benefit?" Mr. Pearce asked. "One nice thing that could come from all of this?"

"Well, I guess there is one positive thing. My father is in love again. Since Mom died, Dad has been lonely. Darleen is good to him, and they seem happy."

"And..." Mr. Pearce encouraged her to continue.

"Well, we are living in a small apartment with hardly any room. Darleen wants us to move into her big country home."

"And..."

"Okay, I have to admit that I've always dreamed of having brothers and sisters. But not like Sherry and Mark."

"So your father is happy and in love. You have the possibility of moving to a better place. And you just may be a bit excited about the idea of having a big family around you."

Emma smiled. The positive sides of the cards were starting to fill up now, and for every negative there was a positive comment to make about what was happening.

ALL IS FAIR IN LOVE AND WAR

Mr. Pearce asked Emma to let down her guard and take a closer look at Darleen and her family. Ignoring the flashy clothes and the makeup, what kind of girl did Emma think Sherry was? Scared, perhaps? Cautious about Emma and her father? Could Sherry just be a normal teenage girl who was confused and missed her father as much as Emma missed her mother? Maybe Emma could get to know the real Sherry before writing her off as odd and hateful. Underneath it all, the two girls did in fact have a lot in common.

And what about Darleen? Emma described her as basically a kind and loving person. Outside of the fact that Darleen was marrying Emma's father, Emma could not really come up with any negative comments about her personally. Emma and Mr. Pearce talked for a few more sessions. On the last day Emma was able to make up a new list, one which she called the Unfair List. Emma decided that she was being unfair in these ways:

- She was not thinking of the happiness of her father.
- She was judging Sherry on her outward appearance before getting to know her.
- She was not giving Darleen a chance to become a new mother to her and a wife to her father.
- She was not thinking of the benefits that Sherry and Mark would have by being raised by her father.

Emma admitted in the end that she did not want her life to change. It was that simple. She did not want to experience another loss, equating the death of her mother to the remarriage of her father. Had she not been able to talk out her feelings, she would have come into the new family with anger and resentment. Her stepsiblings would have responded to her negative attitude, and the family would have been at war from the first day.

But Emma decided to take Mr. Pearce's advice and get to know the members of her new family. She spent time with Mark, helping him with school projects and driving him to his friends' houses when he asked. Since she was the only sibling who had a driver's license, she used that to take Sherry places. Sherry appreciated her stepsister's willingness to make things work in the family. The two girls began to spend time together, and gradually a closeness developed between them. Emma's patience and understanding of her new stepsiblings and stepmother paid off. She was proud of her efforts and especially proud of the results.

Perhaps you carry some of the same feelings that Emma did when she was first struggling with acceptance of her new stepfamily. You may be hurting because your parent is thinking of choosing or has already chosen a new partner. You are faced with the task of adjusting to new faces, new ways of doing things—a new and different life.

Some of you may identify with Katie or Danny or Matthew whom we heard from in this chapter. Try to understand that learning to love and accept new people and new relationships takes time. It may never happen. You may find that although you are living in the same home with your stepfamily, you cannot find it in yourself to love them. Do not be ashamed of those feelings. Love is not something that grows automatically out of a set of circumstances. Love takes time and is built on trust. It is important to remember that it may be just as hard for your stepsiblings to accept and love you as it is for you to accept and love them. It may take months or even years to finally feel comfortable with your new family.

Throughout this chapter we have been talking about the problems and feelings that can arise between stepsiblings when two families come together. There are also many happy and successful stories. Many of you may have had few problems in adjusting. If you were to make a list of the pros and cons you would come up with more positives than negatives about your relationships.

One advantage that many teens wrote about was having additional people in the family who care about you and to whom you can go in time of trouble. It is true that when you aquire new stepsiblings, you also aquire new cousins, aunts, grandparents, etc. You family circle widens, and many close and valuable relationships can be made. Many of the people who described close stepsibling relationships also admitted coming into those relationships with an eagerness to make things work. They said they were willing to accept differences and work around rules that were set up to benefit the new household.

It is a known fact that a loving family provides a nurturing environment for a child. Although you and your stepsiblings have no blood bond to keep your relationship afloat, together you can build one based on trust and friendship. Paula explains:

"I'm nineteen and living in a girl's dorm on campus. It feels just the way it did when my stepsisters first came to live with me. It feels new and exciting. We are like one big family here. All of us have our differences, and quite a bit of arguing goes on. But I know it's not going to last forever. We are all moving on toward different goals. I'm going to enjoy the company and come away with many happy memories of this time."

CHAPTER 4

Jealousy

I t isn't often that parents admit having a favorite among their children. They may admit having a favorite aunt, or cousin, but ask if one of their children is their favorite and you will no doubt hear, "Oh, I love them all equally."

Sometimes, though, long after their kids are out on their own, parents may look back and admit that one of them was the best. "Jenny was the greatest. She was the easiest of all of them to handle." Or, "Ben was the most responsible. If I had to have a favorite, it would be Ben."

During childhood, most parents try to spread their love and attention equally among the children. There are times, however, when somewhere inside a mother or father may admit feeling different toward one particular child, and often that feeling comes out in unconscious gestures (bragging to friends, extra hugs, special gifts).

Mary L., mother of two little girls, said that she always brought home pretty ribbons and bows for her oldest daughter, Sarah, because her hair was long, thick, and wavy. Mary's own hair had always been cut short as a child, and she delighted in the fact that her own daughter had such beautiful hair. She didn't realize that her younger daughter, Brianne, who had thin hair like Mary's, resented the fact that Sarah was rewarded for having beautiful hair. Brianne was angry with her mother for showing what she felt was favoritism, but she took her anger out on her older sister.

Mary recalled a time when Brianne threatened to cut off Sarah's hair with a pair of scissors during an argument. Only then did Mary realize how jealous her younger daughter was and how left out she felt over the special gifts that she brought Sarah. Instead of hair ornaments, Mary decided to bring Brianne something special. She knew that Brianne loved jewelry, and whenever Mary came across a colorful bracelet or child's ring, she surprised Brianne with it. Mary admitted feeling guilty over her daughter's feeling of favoritism, but said she was glad it had been brought to her attention early enough.

It is difficult to treat all children equally when one child excels or stands out among the others, either in looks or achievement. One child may have exceptionally beautiful eyes, or one child may be top student in a class of 300. Often parents cannot help but admire certain qualities in their own children, just at they would someone else's child.

COMPARING

It is one thing to admire a quality or a trait in a child, but a mistake many parents make (myself included) is comparing the child to his brothers or sisters. When negative comparisons are made time and time again, damage can be done to the child's feeling of self-worth. Do any of these questions sound familiar to you?

- Why can't you keep your room clean the way your brother Andrew does?
- Why can't you bring home good grades like your sister Allison?
- Why do I have to ask you three times to do something and your brother Dan only once?
- Why don't you have good eating habits like Marsha?
- Why can't you finish your homework on time like William?

When you hear these questions time after time, it becomes difficult to answer them reasonably. It sounds a bit ridiculous to answer, "You're right, I have terrible eating habits," or "Okay, William is the better person because he finishes his homework before I do." You don't like hearing the comparisons. They sound awful, and they are a blow to the ego.

Sometimes kids who want to be noticed by their parents may decide to adopt a negative role just for the attention. "Oh, she noticed that I'm sloppy," and so he continues to be sloppy and get the same remarks time and time again. He feels that some attention is better than none. The end goal, of course, is winning the parent's favor.

One sixteen-year-old told me that in her family no comparisons or negative remarks are made about one sibling against the other. There is a different means of getting and keeping attention. There are so many kids that they all talk and listen at the same time. She herself has learned not to stop talking, because if she does she loses her parent's attention. They air all their differences in family meetings, but everyone jumps into the discussion because if you lose your chance to speak it could be a while before they come around to you again.

What are some possible answers that you can give when

asked the comparison questions, such as: Why aren't you as neat, smart, good, careful as your brother or sister? Here are some examples:

"But I'm not Andrew. It's true, Andrew likes things in order and always seems to keep his room clean. That's one of my problem areas, just like Andrew's forgetting to bring his homework from school."

"It's true. You do have to ask me to do things more times than you do Dan, but I am busier than he is. He's younger and can take time out immediately to do what you want. I have my after-school job and a lot going on in my life right now. I'm not ignoring you, and I promise I'll do what you ask, but it may not be done as fast as Dan does it."

"Marsha and I have completely different tastes in food. We have always been that way and probably always will be. I can't change the way I eat and the foods I like because of Marsha."

"Ann does bring home good grades, but I think my grades are just as good for *me*. I may not get all As, but I study hard and do the best job I can. I don't like it when you constantly compare me to my sister and how she does in her classes."

Marvin is the father of two boys, Seth, thirteen, and Brent, ten.

"My boys are as opposite as day and night. The oldest is slick. He's also extremely good-looking and very popular in school. Brent, on the other hand, is going through an awkward period. He is shy and sticks pretty much to home. Brent has a few good friends but at this time appears unsure of himself in many situations.

"My wife and I made a concerted effort to give Brent extra love and attention. We felt that he needed it at this time in his life. I remember myself at his age, and we are both quite alike in many respects. I was clumsy and somewhat of a loner. What happened was that our plan backfired. After a while Seth picked up on our attitude toward his brother. He became angry. He also began fighting with his brother. We could not understand the source of his anger until one evening we overheard one of their many arguments. It went something like this:

Seth: What are you so upset about? Mom and Dad will take your side and you know it.

Brent: That's a lie!

Seth: When have they not taken your side? They never listen to anything I have to say.

Brent: You shouldn't complain. You're the hot-shot around here. You can get out of anything.

Seth: Wake up Brent, it's you they care about.

Marvin said that he knew immediately why Seth had been acting the way he had. Looking back over the past months, he realized that Seth was indeed left out much of the time. Seth was in the backround because his parents felt that he had what it took to make it on his own. But Seth was hurt and angry. Marvin saw that they were penalizing Seth for his looks and his confidence. The shift of favoritism ceased immediately.

PLAYING FAVORITES

Identifying with or simply admiring one child should not be confused with favoritism or showing partiality. One child may have traits that the parent admires, such as the ability to forgive or the fortitude to succeed where others have failed.

I admire my younger son for his determination to get something done once he has started it. He may stay up until long after midnight trying to solve a problem or fix a broken toy. He'll exhaust all possibilities trying to get something to work again. I've seen him switching batteries from home appliances into the backs of battery-operated racing cars trying to get them to run.

While I admire his determination, especially for an eight-year-old, I do not let that admiration get in the way of how I treat him in respect to his older brother, who is ten. I try not to give him extra love because he is inquisitive, but I love the fact that he is. Can you see the difference? Not all parents are aware of this difference, however, and outward displays of favoritism are common in many families. This becomes a natural breeding ground for hurt and resentment among the siblings.

There is a big difference between loving people for themselves and loving something unique about them. Think about it. Do you feel that one or perhaps both of your parents favor your sibling over yourself? Try to remember some of the actions or words that made you feel that way. Ask yourself if it is really favoritism that is being shown, or just admiration for a certain quality or characteristic that your brother or sister has. Was he or she commended for a personal achievement? Complimented on a job well done? What you think is a show of favoritism may really be just a nod of approval or a heartfelt acknowledgment. It may look as though the sibling is loved more than you, but in reality they may be saying, "Good for you," or "Congratulations on a job well done." That does not imply that your sibling is better than you, or more loved, or comes first on your parents' list and you are at the bottom.

It isn't likely that a child will say of his parents, "Dad works harder than Mom. He is taller and has more money than she does. Dad's the best in my eyes; I love him better than Mom." In all probability you do recognize certain characteristics of each parent, but you don't choose which is going to receive the bulk of your love. You notice and admire different qualities in each of them, but you love them both as your parents.

Feelings of favoritism occur in most families at one time or another. Usually, though, kids are favored on different days, or perhaps at different periods of their lives, so that as a whole no child clearly prevails.

Many parents go through a period when one child seems the easiest to handle. For weeks one son or daughter may be sweet and loving and the days pass by without incident. But there are also periods when one child goes through a difficult stage. Each day becomes a battle, over clothes, friends, rules of the house. This child may be moody and obstinate, and nothing you can do or say will lift the mood until it passes. It isn't difficult for a parent to favor the good child and feel anger and, yes, sometimes hate toward the troublesome child.

This applies to sibling relationships as well. One brother or sister may be sweet and kind to you, while the other is abusive. The sweet one becomes your favorite, while the other becomes your least favorite.

FEELINGS OF FAVORITISM
CAN AFFECT SELF-WORTH

Often the sibling who is consistently left out or ignored either by parents or other siblings tends to have low self-esteem. Many confusing feelings come to the surface. If you feel this way, you may be asking:

- Why do they like the others better than me?
- Why am I not included as he or she is?
- What I have I done to offend them?
- How can I make them love me as much as my brother or sister?

You may feel that no matter how hard you try you count less than your sibling in your parents' eyes. First, and most important, realize that you are not alone with these feelings. Many teens say that they felt they were loved less than their siblings, and quite a few did not understand what was going on in their parents' minds when they displayed this favoritism. Some say that they found themselves trying too hard to be liked by their sibling. They say that they were always the one to make up first in a fight, that they protected their sibling against others but that the feelings or actions were never reciprocated.

Marlene explains:

"In my situation, I was forever trying to get my older sister to notice me. We are only two years apart, but for some reason she avoided me like I had some sort of contagious disease. I tried so hard to get her to like me, even to the point of ignoring my own needs. If I had $10 I'd buy her a little gift, something that I knew she would like. I was always trying to get her approval, but she never loved me in return.

"Now that we are both through with college and out on our own, I see that our relationship has not changed much. If I don't call her I never hear from her. Once I asked my mother why my sister didn't like me, and she said it was because she didn't know how to show her love. I am a giving type of person and display my affection outwardly. My mother said that my sister didn't know how to reach out to people. She said that when we were both growing up I was really her favorite, but she never let it show. Both my mother and I agree that it is hard to keep loving someone who gives nothing in return."

Our feelings of self-worth can truly be affected by the way others treat us. We may be able to give love, but when it is not accepted or returned we start to feel, What's the use? Why keep trying when I know nothing will come of this? Some may actually question whether they are good enough or lovable enough or worthy. The answer is *Yes*. The problem does not lie with you; it lies with the person who does not respond for one reason or another. Do not question your own integrity or your own worthiness just because of another's behavior.

If you do for a person and care for a person and really love that person but find that it is a one-way street, maybe it is time to stop trying so hard.

This is often evident in boyfriend/girlfriend relationships, where one is always the giver and the other is the taker. The boy loves the girl deeply. He calls her and sends her notes and letters. He buys her gifts and sends her cards on every holiday. But she does none of this in return. She plays it cool and is passive in this one-sided relationship— until the boy stops being the giver. He may decide that he's interested in someone else. The cards and letters cease. The phone calls become fewer. And then the girl starts to take notice. She thinks, maybe I should have done this or maybe I should have said that. It could be too late for her. Her appreciation for the boy's love and attention may come too late, because the boy has lost interest.

The same scenario can be applied to one-sided sibling relationships. If you find yourself, as Marleen did, giving of yourself time and time again with nothing in return, do not feel that something is wrong with *you*. You are loving and giving, but the other person does not respond. Try to understand why. Perhaps something is wrong in his or her life that no one knows about. But if, after repeated attempts, you cannot break through, realize that the problem lies with that person and that you are just as worthy and as good as you always were.

THOSE SIBLING BONDS

We've talked about jealousy and about favoritism and read some personal experiences on the subject. Let's talk now about coping procedures. What can we do when these situations arise? How can we learn to better understand and deal with feelings of being left out or overlooked by our parents in favor of another siblings?

Let's remember that what we are dealing with is *family*. These are close, private, personal relationships unlike any others. They are not like friendships that can be broken or ignored or that you may or may not decide to mend. You cannot walk away from a sibling relationship totally. You have to face the problems and deal with them.

Brothers and sisters share a sibling bond, an invisible bond that separates them from all other relationships. Just as in best-friend relationships, if one sibling seems to have it all—the looks, the grades, the friends—it is difficult for the other to have to sit back and applaud and say, "That's great." "I'm happy for you." "Bravo." Inside you are really thinking, "Okay, enough already. What about me? When will it be my turn to shine?"

First and most important, realize that it is normal to have these feelings. When one brother or sister is always out front, your own smile begins to fade. You may even secretly wish that things would go badly for the other. Don't blame that person; it is not his or her fault. Try not to take out your frustration on your sibling or let your anger or envy rule. Perhaps you want to talk to your parents or even your sibling about your feelings but are embarrassed or at a loss for words.

Following are sample conversations that might help you get started.

"Judy, don't laugh when I tell you this, but I am jealous of you because you always get better grades than I do. It seems that if I get Cs, you get Bs. If I bring home Bs, you bring home As. Mom and Dad make a big deal over your exams and report cards, but they hardly comment on mine. I'm really proud that you are doing so well in school, but I feel as if we are in a contest and I'm always the loser. That is why I have been acting the way I have toward you lately."

"Dad, I'm not sure if you are even aware of this, but you have taken Brian to four out of the last six hockey games. I like hockey too, and I get angry when Brian is always is chosen to go with you. I feel as if you almost prefer Brian over me."

"Stephanie, I know you've been told this many times, but you have terrific taste in clothes. Everything looks well on you. I wish I could wear clothes the way you do. When I get angry because you want to borrow my things, it's because I secretly wish I looked the way you do in them. It bothers me when I see you getting compliments wearing my things. They are compliments that I would like to get but don't."

Describe your feelings, don't judge. Acknowledge that the problem may be with you. Start by explaining:

"I want you to know that I am upset because..."
"I envy the way you skate with ease..."
"I'm feeling down because you were picked to go fishing with Dad..."

You may feel silly saying it, but in a sense you are being totally honest. That is the way you feel. You may want to lash out at your brother or sister, but try to substitute a message instead. It is better than hurling insults, directing blame, or swallowing anger.

ASSESSING THE SITUATION

Next time you start to feel pangs of jealousy or resentment toward your sibling, stop and ask yourself questions:

- Could I be overreacting in my feelings?
- Can I find it in myself to be happy for my sibling's accomplishments?
- Am I directing anger and hostility at my brother or sister for something that is not his or her fault?
- Have I gone to my parents with my feelings and brought them to their attention?

Many teens say that they wanted some sort of revenge for what they felt was favoritism shown toward other siblings.

You may even find yourself thinking negative thoughts about your brothers and sisters, such as wishing them harm or wishing that they would vanish and leave you to be the only or favored child in your parents' eyes. Do not be ashamed of those feelings. They are just a message from you, saying, "Hey, I want to be noticed too."

Twins have the very same feeling. Often one twin will imagine that the other is gone from the family and he or she is the only child left to reap love and attention from the parents.

A friend who is now forty once told me that when he was twelve he used to imagine that he was suddenly an orphan. He remembers imagining that he was adopted by his TV heroes, Roy Rogers and Dale Evans, and was known as their only cherished son. He laughs about it now, but during that time of rivalry with his sisters and fighting with his parents, this dream carried him through the lonely spots.

Try to see the situation for what it really is, to recognize where the anger and hostility is coming from.

ADMITTING FEELINGS

Deep down in your heart you know that you love your brother or sister. However, you may rarely show those feelings. Why? Sometimes you may be more concerned with how your sibling makes *you* feel than with how your sibling actually feels. Think about it. Do you constantly question his or her words or actions and think, "He's making my life miserable." "He makes me feel awful." "She's ruined my day with her bragging or her bad mood."

Turn it around for a moment and ask yourself, "But how did I make her feel today? Have I been whining or complaining lately? Is she angry with the way I have been acting?" It's a two-way street, and negative emotions are experienced on both sides. Think of a recent time when your sibling has been hostile to you, when you haven't seen a smile or received a friendly word for days. Look back and decide if that mood could possibly be a reflection of your negative actions.

Realize also that brothers and sisters do have a tendency to deal with each other solely in terms of power: What are you taking away from me? What can I get back from you? After months or years of arguing, trust breaks down and the relationship becomes a series of battles. People often lose sight of the fact that the ones we are pushing away are the ones we really love and care about the most.

It is not a crime to admit feelings of hate and despair and envy and love. What is confusing about many of those feelings is that they may be felt at the same time toward the same person. You hate your brother for breaking your tape recorder, but at the same time you feel bad because he is only seven and he didn't do it on purpose. You are angry at him because it will take time and money to repair it, yet you know that you still love him and have to accept his apology.

MIXED FEELINGS OF LOVE AND HATE

Even though you may be fighting bitterly and have angry thoughts about your sibling, somewhere inside you know that you care about what is happening. You care about hurt egos, insults, and physical confrontations. You may cry and scream or sulk and ignore your sibling, but there is something within you that you cannot ignore. That is the fact that alongside this so-called hate you are feeling, there is also a feeling of love. And that is what is so confusing.

How, you may ask, can one love and hate someone at the

same time? Easy. You love your younger sister because she is a part of you. You are growing up together in the same household and are sharing many experiences and building memories for the future. You have been with her through good times and bad. She is family, and you know that you would come to her defense in a minute against any outsider who might want to give her a bad time.

But at the same time, you may be hating her too, because she got you in trouble or she knows how to make you miserable in fifty different ways. Because of her you have been grounded. Because of her you have been angry, embarrassed in front of others, annoyed. You absolutely hate the things she does, the way she acts, and her values or opinions. But somewhere in the middle of this hate and anger is a soft spot. You know that if someone outside your family started telling you how awful your sister is, you would be the first one to come to her defense. She is, after all, your sister, and although *you* may be able to say bad things about her, heaven help the person who harbors those very same thoughts or feelings. You know that if she is ill or hurting you will be there for her. Because you love her.

Adults feel this love/hate emotion as well. The young mother is at her wit's end. Her toddler has a bad cold and has been awake all night. Today he is whining and cranky and there is nothing the mother can do to make him feel better. He's been crying and screaming and throwing things on the floor. The mother's nerves are shot. She feels she cannot stand another minute of the noise. She looks at her baby with his nose running, his soiled clothes and angry face, and thinks, "I hate you. I hate you this moment for your fussiness, for your crying, for the fact that you kept me up all night and I'm exhausted." And then the mother starts to cry herself.

But as she cries and feels this anger and resentment, she is picking up her baby and cleaning him up. She is holding him and rocking him and kissing away his tears. Because he is her baby and she loves him. At that moment she is loving him and hating him at the same time.

The same is true of many teenagers. How often have you heard stories of teenagers running away from home? They live on the streets, and some resort to crime, often ending up in jail. But time after time they are bailed out by their parents and end up back at home. Their parents scream at them and tell them how rotten they are, but they keep bailing them out and bringing them back home. Why? Because their parents love them. They hate what they are doing to themselves and to the family, but there is an underlying bond that cannot be severed.

Love and hate are very strong emotions, but they are not as opposite as you may think. Some experts feel that to hate someone strongly you must have some feeling for the person first. Otherwise you would not care at all; you would feel indifference.

If a friend slighted you and her friendship did not mean much, you would probably walk away and not look back. But if you found yourself seething in anger, and telling yourself how much you hate her, and wanting to tell her how angry you are, the relationship may mean more to you than you realize. Her actions and your feelings have touched a strong emotional response. You may hate her for what she did, but you have good feelings about her as a friend. Being angry is worth the effort. Because you care.

"I despise my older brother and said that I would never speak to him again. We both are now in our thirties, and since our fight more than ten years ago I have held to my word. I tell anyone who will listen how much I hate him, but the fact is, every year at Christmas I wait around the phone thinking that he might call. I am stubborn, and I know I will not be the first to break the ice. I swear that I will never forgive him, but if he should call tomorrow, I think I would cry."

Edith, 35

"I tend to run my home like an army camp, and sometimes my kids pay the price. With five under fourteen, we have to have some type of order system. In the beginning I set specific times for everything, dinner at 6, homework at 7:30, lights out by 9.

All the kids had to abide by those rules as well as others that I had written down and had them memorize. The oldest ones complained the most, especially about having lights out by 9. The youngest was never hungry at dinner because she had late naps and snacked late in the afternoon.

If one wanted to go to the market with me, I took them all. My middle one hated going to the market, but I dragged him along because it was easier for me. The baby never liked caramel apples, so I never brought them home for the others.

Eventually I realized that all the fighting among the kids was brought on by me and my strict rules. What I was not doing was listening to the specific needs of each child.

They were bitter against their siblings because one's likes or dislikes affected the whole group. They were angry with the baby because she didn't like caramel apples and they did. They insisted that she ask for them so they could get them too.

When I saw what was happening, I tried to change

my way of doing things. It wasn't easy. But I saw that it wasn't fair to make the fourteen-year-old have lights out by 9, nor was it fair to drag my middle one to the market when he didn't want to go. I realized that I was not treating them as individuals. The change did not come about immediately. But after a time the rivalry began to settle down and their relationships improved.

It has been very difficult for me. I have to juggle many schedules and deal with five distinct personalities. But I know my change was for the better. I am hoping that in the long run I will see the results of my efforts."

Carleen, 39

"I have one sister (older). She is very pretty and does better in school than I do. We compete in every way and base our success on who gets more: attention, friends, grades, praise. She is better in school, but she is a brat and does not have many friends.

I am jealous of her because of her success in school. I paint, something that my sister cannot do. My paintings hang in our den, and when people notice, my sister always laughs and rolls her eyes, saying, 'Oh, my little sister did those.' I think it all kind of evens out. To me, we are equal in our successes, and that kind of keeps the peace."

Kim, 15

IN SUMMARY

After reading this chapter on jealousy and favoritism, it is hoped that you will put into practice some of what has been said. It is important to realize that the majority of sibling fighting starts with feelings of jealousy and favoritism. It is natural to be envious of a brother or sister who seems to get all the attention, and it is not easy always to be happy for a sibling who does better than we do.

Here is a summarization of some important points to remember:

- Try to recognize the difference between admiration for a sibling's accomplishments or characteristics and actual favoritism.
- When your parents constantly compare you to your brother or sister, explain to them that the comparison bothers you. Point out your good points and the fact that there is a difference between your sibling and you and probably always will be. You are two separate individuals.
- Do not take out feelings of anger or jealousy on your sibling. Realize that it is not his or her fault, but explain your feelings to your sibling and to your parents.
- Be happy for your sibling's accomplishments just as you would want him or her to be happy for you. Do not hold back praise because it is something that you wish you had done.
- Understand that love/hate feelings toward brothers or sisters are common. Differentiate between anger and hate over something that has been said or done and anger and hate of the person.

Feelings of jealousy and favoritism can stand in the way of close sibling relationships. Don't you agree that it is a waste of precious time to keep a brother or sister at a distance because of something he or she has and you don't have? Let go of those envious feelings. It is time to change and time to grow.

When a person grows, he gives up an old way of seeing himself. Part of the growing comes from realizing that you have been dishonest with yourself, and that realization can motivate you to change.

Think it over. Go over some of your past feelings of being left out, of jealousy of a sibling. Ask yourself if it really is that big a deal if your brother is quicker or more coordinated or better in sports than you are. Can you find it in yourself to be happy for him too?

No parent or child is perfect, nor is any of us likely to be, and so all of us are at one time or another deeply involved in uncertainty over love and being loved. Try not to tie yourself down with nagging thoughts about not being loved or endless questions such as: Why can't I be like my sister? Why don't I look like my brother? Learn to love and accept your brother and sister for who they are, and learn to feel worthy just because you are you.

CHAPTER 5

Conflict and

Quarrels

The tension was so thick you could cut it with a knife. Each boy stood facing the other, face red and grimacing in anger. Fists were clenched and bobbed out in front. The referee stood on the outside trying to defuse the situation, but the fighters ignored him and came in closer, taunting each other to throw the first punch. It was Saturday evening at the boxing matches, right? Not quite. It was Saturday evening at the O'Malleys' and the two older sons were just seconds away from knocking each other down.

Their father, the referee, tried to intervene, first pulling one son aside, then standing between them. In the backround their mother was pleading for them to stop. Shattered dishes from the dinner table littered the floor.

Phil lunged at Frank and hit him square in the face. Frank returned the punch and missed. Phil connected again, and now their mother intervened, screaming for them to stop. The whole family was involved, but Phil and Frank kept at it, each vowing to get the other before the fight was over.

What could have caused this violent outbreak in the O'Malley family? Why did Phil and Frank resort to physical fighting, rather than verbal abuse? For these two brothers, it had been a buildup of many days of anger and frustration. Trouble had started weeks earlier when Phil had made a play for Frank's longtime girlfriend, Vanessa. Vanessa had been planning to break up with Frank anyway, and decided that she liked Phil and wanted to date him.

Frank was livid, but he was too hurt and embarrassed to admit it to his brother. Instead, he brooded about it and barely spoke to Phil or anyone else in the family.

Phil knew that Frank was angry and tried a few times to talk with him. Nothing worked. Frank slammed doors in Phil's face and met his brother's attempts at conversation with stony silence.

Meanwhile, Phil and Vanessa continued to date. At first they dated behind Frank's back because they knew how upset he was. After a time, however, Phil became angry that he couldn't be seen in his own home with his girlfriend. Frank and Vanessa began dating openly, and they started to tease Frank about his jealousy, trying to use humor to defuse the situation.

When that didn't work, Phil decided to shut Frank out completely. Both brothers walked around in silence, each telling himself over and over what he would really like to tell the other. The boys were heading for trouble. First there were angry looks between them, then abusive name-calling, and soon they were involved in shoving matches. Not long afterward came the showdown that erupted into physical violence and threatened to send both of them to the hospital.

This occurs in many homes. Siblings who have lost the power to communicate end up hurting each other. It can start by teasing, but if that is not stopped or worked out, before long fists are flying.

Many different behaviors provoke physical altercations:

- Jealousy
- Criticism
- Name-calling
- Teasing
- Antagonizing

TEASING CAN BE CRUEL

All of us at one time or another have teased someone or been teased. Siblings tease each other constantly. You tease a brother about a bad haircut; he teases you about falling down. Younger siblings tease older siblings about girlfriends and boyfriends. Older siblings tease younger ones about sucking their thumb or wetting the bed. Usually this type of teasing is meant innocently, but nevertheless it hurts. If it is done in a malicious way, such as teasing about pimples, braces, or being skinny, it can be a source of anger and embarrassment.

When siblings tease you about something personal, they know that they are striking a sensitive nerve. They may continue on and on until you decide that you've had enough. Your siblings may feel in control when they see you wince or cry or stand up in anger. They are getting a response.

How do you react to a sibling who teases you? The following are answers to that question from teens who were surveyed:

- I walk away and start doing something. My brother usually won't follow me. I won't give him the satisfaction of answering him.
- If my sister teases me about my frizzy hair (which she always does), I find something about her that I don't like and give it back to her in the next sentence (usually about her freckles).
- I end up hitting my younger brother when he doesn't let up. I'll take it for a few minutes but not much longer.
- I scream and tell him to be quiet, but in stronger terms.
- If it is something about me personally I'll feel bad about it for days. I hate to be teased by anyone.
- I ignore it, but when the time is right it will be her turn to get it.

ACT NOW!

It is important to examine closely how your own thoughts and feelings and actions affect your total response to teasing. Do you react with humor? Do you retaliate with physical force? Does it bounce off your shoulder without a second thought?

For most of us a reaction is necessary. We must respond to someone taunting or criticizing us. But how?

One way to catch people off guard after they have said something to you is to *ask for more information*. "I'm ignorant about this. In what way? Explain how you came to this conclusion." Don't accept a negative statement. Ask for more details. Ask whether they are joking, and if not, can they be more specific? In other words, put them on the spot. Request an explanation of what they have said.

"You look awful in your braces. Don't smile! You'll blind us with that metal gleam."

"What do you mean by awful? You know I don't have a choice; I have to wear them for two years. How will it bother you, really, if I smile?

"What an idiot! Can't you read the directions to see how this works?"

"I've never put one of these together before. Is that what you mean when you call me an idiot, because I didn't know how to do this on the first try?"

If you are on the receiving end of negative comments and ridicule, don't throw up your hands in despair or walk away and pretend to ignore the situation. Throw the ball back to the person who is teasing or making the insult. Be specific. Ask what it is that the person doesn't like or ask him to be more detailed about his comment.

Don't come on in an intimidating manner, because the person will immediately become defensive and the minor altercation may escalate. Make it sound as if you really want help in understanding exactly what the person is saying. *Ask for a solution.*

One way to defuse the situation would be to ask calmly, "What would you do about this if you were in my place?" That implies that you are open for discussion, something that the teaser probably was not planning on. You may find him squirming and somewhat embarrassed.

You are so off-key! Listen to your voice, it sounds terrible. (laughing) Maybe you should leave the singing to me and mouth the words.

Oh? What should the correct key sound like? Can you sing it so I can see where I am making the mistake?

If it is the class bully who says this to you and he has a

crowd of buddies around him, getting a laugh at your expense, the last thing he wants to hear is a request for his help. The same is true in sibling relationships. Your first impulse may be to strike out at your brother or sister, but instead start by explaining. "I want you to know that I am extremely upset. What you said hurt me." Then ask questions. Talk *with*, not *at* your sibling. Learning to tolerate teasing or consistent criticism from a sibling is easier when we know how to deal with it.

ROCK THE BOAT!

Many of us are afraid to express our true feelings to our siblings. That is especially true when the feeling is anger. People think, "If you get angry I'll know you don't love me," and so they walk away on tiptoes, afraid to make waves. Sometimes you may think, "If I tell them what I am thinking, if I expose my thoughts, they will laugh or look at me like I'm crazy, and then it will be even worse." They could very well stare at you in disbelief if you approach them instead of walking away as you have always done. They may not be ready to face you or communicate with you. They liked it the old way when they were in control. This was not part of the plan.

Switch places and imagine how you would feel if you were making a negative comment in jest to your brother and sister. How would you react if they walked up to you and asked you to explain your comment? Okay, what now? They were suppose to *take* it, not *talk* about it. In fact, you may be shuffling your feet and feeling embarrassed. You have been put on the spot. You may even think twice another time because you don't want to have to explain yourself to your siblings.

EXPRESSING ANGER

An important point to realize about anger is that it can be healthy and constructive. It is a form of communication. Anger is an expression of your *needs*. Expressing anger can actually improve your relationship with your sibling. It is phony to pretend that nothing your sibling does bothers you.

Simply ignoring brothers and sisters who incessantly tease or criticize you will make your life miserable. If you can't confront them and clear the air, you end up walking around muttering to yourself about what you should have said, or what you are going to say next time. It sounds great when you say it to yourself, but you know it is frustrating because you cannot get up the nerve to tell them to their faces how angry you are or how much something bothers you.

The longer you hold your anger in, the worse it will be. It will smolder and grow until one day it is released in a vast explosion of temper and harsh words. Anything can light the fuse, but once it has been ignited weeks or months of unspoken words can be released.

It does not have to be that way. Once you know that anger is not bad or wrong, you will realize that it doesn't always have to be displayed by screaming or by violence. That only happens when you have held it in for so long that it finally boils over.

One reason we hold angry thoughts inside is because we do not want to make waves or rock the boat.

"He called me stupid in front of my friend. Then he pulled my chair out and I fell on the floor. He got a big laugh. I didn't tell him how furious I was with him because I didn't want to start something."

Reuben, 14

"My older brother took his friend into my room, and together they went through my tape collection. I walked in and was so angry because they did not bother to ask my permission. But I just walked out and was mad at myself for not having the guts to tell them I didn't like what they were doing. I burned about it for days but never said anything to my brother. I didn't want to start a fight."

Matt, 16

Chances are that Matt's brother will continue to invade his privacy, because Matt has never said anything about it. If he had taken his brother aside that same evening and explained how upset and angry he was, his brother would have known that Matt would feel the same way if it should happen again.

If you say nothing about your feelings or do not speak up, the other person will get the message that:

- I can do it again.
- It doesn't seem to bother him.
- I got a laugh at his expense and it didn't get me in trouble.

You are making it easy for the person by letting him or her get away with it. But if you react to the action or comment with your honest emotion—anger, disgust, hurt—you are stating that the action will elicit a response from you each and every time. And once your emotion is released, you will feel much better.

When emotion is held back, that old scary feeling starts to build up inside, often taking on physical manifestations such as a pounding heart or an intense headache. You may have sleepless nights, tossing and turning over emotions that are kept locked inside.

Try to remember a time when you were embarrassed or angry about something negative said to you by a sibling. How did you feel? Were there things that you wanted to say but didn't? Say out loud now everything you wish you could have said.

- You made me cry and I'm mad at you.
- I want to slap you for what you said about me.
- How dare you call me those names? Take a look at yourself!
- You were 100% wrong in what you said.
- You owe me an apology.

What do you notice about those statements? Most of them begin with the word "You." And that is natural because you are retaliating: "*You* are wrong. *You* are to blame." You are pointing your finger at the person who made the statement and accusing him or her of doing something. The person then has a natural reaction, and that is to say, "*I* did not. *I* am not." He or she immediately goes on the defensive. Think for a moment of someone saying to you, *You* are wrong or *You* caused this to happen. What would your response be? *I* did not! And then comes the battle of—*You* did so! *I* did not! *You* did so! The main issue gets lost in the accusations, and it becomes a battle of wills.

What if you were to drop the "You" message and state an "I" message?

- I am angry because you told our secret.
- I am not sure you understood my point.
- I am tired of hearing you call me that.

Expressing your feelings directly without projecting blame gives the other person a chance to communicate his or her feelings or to give you a rational explanation about a comment or an action. By taking the softer (but firm and direct) approach, you will be better able to get to the root of the problem and stop it from happening again.

FOCUS ON THE PROBLEM

Sometimes when you are very angry with your brother or sister it is easy to go off on a tangent about other things done in the past. You begin thinking of other times and situations when you were mad at him or her and you bring those things to the present, which makes you even angrier.

- I'm so mad that she borrowed my sweater without asking. And come to think of it, last month she took my earrings. Why, even this past Christmas she used my new skates before I had a chance to use them myself!
- He dripped ice cream all over my new carpet. Wait until he gets home from school! He's so irresponsible, I'm going to let him have a piece of my mind about all the bad things he's done lately.

If your little brother lies to you, don't be mad at him because he also stole $5 from you two years ago. Address the issue of the moment. "I am upset because you listened in on my phone conversation. You know I wouldn't do that to you. It is an invasion of my privacy. I am not going to say anything to Mom and Dad, but I hope it won't happen again."

You will feel frustrated and probably silly saying that, especially in a matter-of-fact way. But at least you said it. In a few short sentences you told your sibling that you were aware of what he did, that you were hurt or angered by it, and that you expect it not to happen again.

After you have said it, don't wait for a grand-scale apology or a tearful admission of guilt. Don't expect much of any reply. Be content with just an "Okay" or a nod. Then drop the subject. If you keep harping on the issue or resort to using "You" messages, the situation can escalate into a far worse scenario. Realize that you will not hurt your sibling's feelings by standing up for yourself. It is possible for you to disagree about something and still live together with affection and respect.

HOW DOES OUR BEHAVIOR AFFECT THE FAMILY?

As we have seen, fighting among siblings is quite normal. How you each enter into these altercations and how you come out varies with each individual. When disagreements escalate into full-fledged war, your parents intervene and the whole family becomes involved. There are harsh words, whining, accusations, and bitterness.

Many dinner hours are sat through in silence, members brooding over ongoing disputes. It may take a family days or weeks to recover from an emotional sibling battle. Tensions run high. Egos are shattered. Often siblings who are not involved in the conflict are affected by it. They see and hear what is going on. Parents are forced to take sides, they begin punishing, and the total mood of the family plummets to an all-time low.

Erick explains:

"If fighting is going on between myself and my sixteen-year-old brother, everybody suffers. Mom refuses to cook for us if we have been at it all day. She says that she wants to sit at the table in peace, not listen to us air our differences. In a way I don't blame her, because our differences end up in kicking and wrestling matches. Neither one of us will give up first. But long after we have made up and are friends, Mom is still angry, and we have to joke around with her and beg her to sit down with us again."

Helene says:

"When my sister and I go at it, we always end up getting grounded. Dad is the one who punishes us. Our mother is sick with a severe muscle disease. She is in bed most of the time. We try not to argue in the house because we don't want to disturb her. We do most of our yelling and screaming at each other out-side. Even if the fight starts in the house, we have to hold everything in and settle it later. Sometimes the tension gets unbearable. By the time we settle our argument, we are almost ready to kill each other . It just builds up inside us and that makes it worse."

Some parents jump into every sibling argument and try to settle it themselves. Others ignore their kids' fighting until it starts to get violent. There are parents who yell and scream themselves, and those that try to have their kids work out their own differences. It is important to realize that parents react differently to sibling conflicts at different stages in their own life. They may be going through a rough period, such as the loss of a job, or a divorce. At the time you are fighting, they may be under tremendous pressure and stress.

When siblings fight, it may become unbearable for parents and they may overreact in anger and rage. At a different time in their life, however, they may react differently, more calmly, to the same argument.

How many times can you remember your own parents reacting to your arguments in a way that completely surprised you? They may have been soft-spoken and understanding when you expected them to come down hard. Or they may have reacted strongly to a simple discussion you were having with your sister. Parents have their good days and their bad days just as you do. Their response to your conflict may well reflect their mood or state of mind at the time.

So it is up to you to handle a conflict with your brother or sister. Do not expect your parents always to be there to intervene. Learn how to deal with your own reactions and your own responses.

Yes, your behavior, your sibling altercations and differences do affect others in the family. You may settle a disagreement with your brother, but long afterward tension in the house remains. It may take longer for others to forget what you have forgotten.

It is important, then, to assume responsibility for settling your conflicts. Talk them over in the morning before school or after dinner when there is time. Try not to bring other siblings into the matter. Learn to think and to act on your own, negotiating your own settlements with your siblings. That is a major step toward independence and growth.

THE TRUTH ABOUT ANGER

What happens when you get so angry with your sibling that you fear what you might end up doing? When you are afraid that you will have to resort to violence to end the conflict? That happens in many cases; simple discussions heat up and end up with one or both persons getting injured.

Perhaps that has happened to you. You may have been

so angry with your sibling for so long that one day it exploded into a physical altercation. You may have experienced it many times and not known how to control it or prevent it. Violent outbursts can be controlled. The following steps may help you next time you feel angry enough to explode:

- Immediately focus on something else or someone else in the house. Try to divert your attention elsewhere for a few minutes to give yourself time to calm down.
- Count to ten slowly before making any move. Take deep relaxing breaths, and try to regain control of your emotions.
- Ask yourself if it is worth getting hurt or hurting your sibling over this matter. Do you really want to risk coming out of this with a black eye or bruised arm or risk giving the same to your sibling?

Dr. Evan Koursh is a physician on the staff at Cedars Sinai Hospital in Los Angeles, specializing in pediatric medicine and general practice. Dr. Koursh says:

"As a medical professional, my advice for teens is *communication*. Fighting among siblings never resolves a conflict; it only flares tempers and causes people to say things they often regret and that may have irreparable consequences.

"It is especially important for the teens (or parents) to recognize when a discussion becomes a fight. At that time a 'cooling-off' interval is needed, since that is when even rational individuals forget why the argument began. Their only goal is to win even it it hurts the other person. Name-calling, tattling, accusing all serve to thwart the process of communication.

"Another important concept is the 'hidden agenda'. Often it is difficult for the involved parties to recognize that their argument may be based on a completely separate matter. Looking at *why* one is really mad at a sibling (or a parent or a friend) can allow discovery of the true heart of many fights. Hurt feelings from a past event are a common cause for subsequent fights over seemingly unconnected occurrences."

It's up to you. Realize that by taking ownership of your feelings you can start to choose how you will react to something or how you will feel. When you are angry and believe that others or outside events are controlling how you feel, you have little choice in the matter.

Letting Others Control	*Controlling Own Feelings*
Because of the RAIN, we are inside fighting all day.	I have been playing cards with you for three hours. It's too long, and we need to break. I'm tired.
Don't speak to me. I'm in a bad mood because my TEACHER gave me an F on my math test.	I'm angry with myself because I didn't study for my math test.
SHE makes me feel awful because of her attitude.	I feel depressed when she brags about how much she has.
I overeat because MOM brings home too many snacks.	I have poor self-control and cannot help snacking even though I know I don't need the extra calories.
ROSS makes me mad when he brags about his grades in school.	I get mad at myself for letting Ross's statements about his grades get to me.

Resolving sibling conflicts basically involves developing an understanding between you and your siblings, making sure that you know what you can expect from each other, what is acceptable and what is not acceptable.

Can they interrupt you and get away with it? Can you criticize them without angry retaliation? You all know what makes the others angry or which buttons to press to get a certain response.

The important thing for each of you to do is to make those feelings known. State them as you feel them, and it will make it easier for you in the next confrontation. If you feel that you were unjustly criticized by your older brother in front of your boyfriend and you were embarrassed—tell him *how* embarrassed you were. Tell him that you'd appreciate his being more considerate in the future, that in the future you'd like him to come to you privately when he has something negative to say. He may do the very same thing again, and you may have to explain again. But don't ignore it even if you have to come back a third time. He will eventually realize that you do not like it, and he may begin to think twice before doing it again.

Hiding your anger will not solve the problem. If anything, it will make it worse. How can your brother know that you were embarrassed if you don't tell him? How can your sister know that you feel awful when she laughs at you during ice skating lessons?

It is important to tell the person just how angry you are and to defuse a future confrontation.

A LETTER FROM THOMAS

"After years of trying, my parents were told that they were unable to have children. They adopted my older brother. Three years later my mother became pregnant and I was born. I'm told that my brother was a 'problem child' from infancy. He continued to be so, although I'm certain that some of his problems centered around the fact that he was adopted and I was the natural child.

"We fought often while growing up, though having no other siblings I'm not sure whether our fights were any more frequent or severe than those of other brothers. I do remember being beaten up a lot. At the time I felt terrorized. My parents would leave us at home together, and eventually he would threaten to kill me. I would lock myself in a room and he would break the door down. We went through a lot of doors back then.

"One of our major differences was scholastic. My brother had a moderately severe learning disability at a time when schools were teaching reading by rote memorization. That only compounded his problem. I had a pretty easy time in school, and I remember once feeling very close to my brother when he asked me to help him with his homework. It was one of the few times I've felt close to him.

"There were actually a few advantages in our being so different. Because of my brother's behavioral problems, teachers, family, and friends began to expect the worst of him. When I came along, my misbehavior was so minor in comparison to his that it was often overlooked. That only served to make him more angry; as he saw it, he was blamed for everything and I escaped unscathed whether I had misbehaved or not.

"Now that we are adults, my brother and I get along pretty well, but I would not describe our relationship as close. We no longer fight (verbally or physically), but we have little in common and our conversations are somewhat forced. I think he still harbors great resentment toward me, although I think that those feelings are focused toward my parents. In his mind, they gave me every advantage and denied him much. From my viewpoint, they offered him help and support throughout the years but were disappointed so often that they tired of supporting him.

"The angriest I've been with my brother are the times he has created such havoc with the family that it induced physical illness in my parents. The closest I've felt to my brother is now, when we can sit down as two adults and rationally talk about what went on in our childhood, how we felt about it then, and how we feel about it now."

ASK FOR OUTSIDE HELP IF YOU NEED IT

Daily sibling arguments and bickering may get to you after a while. All of us have our tolerance level, our breaking point, so to speak. Everyone who has siblings has felt troubled and angry with their brothers and sisters. It's a fact of life—you live together, you argue, you make up. When the fighting gets out of hand and you can't take it anymore, you have it out, either with your siblings or by bringing your parents into it.

But if your battles just seem to be getting worse, if they are becoming physical in nature, if you are having negative thoughts about your sibling more than just once in a while, you may need to reach out for expert help. The mental health profession consists of counselors, psychologists, social workers, and psychiatrists, people who are experienced in handling such problems. Do not be embarrassed to seek one out. A therapist will not laugh at you or make you feel uncomfortable. You will not be hypnotized or made to do or say anything that makes you feel bad or wrong. He or she will simply talk and listen, and what you say will be kept strictly confidential. A therapist who is trained in family conflict will teach you the art of negotiation and show you how to see your problems in a new way.

Some of you may feel funny about going to a counselor for help. You may see it as a sign of weakness or feel guilty for telling someone else your family problems. Realize that asking for help indicates that you have courage and strength. You want things to be better for you and those you love. Asking for help says that you are willing to take charge of your life.

Your own doctor knows qualified people you can talk to. School counselors can make recommendations. Therapists have a way of seeing through egos, behind feelings, and pinpointing the areas of trouble. Do not hesitate to seek outside help if you feel you need it.

IN SUMMARY

Just as parents are asked to respect their children, so are siblings asked to respect each other. We don't go out of our way to start disagreements. We don't sit and think of ways to make our siblings angry. These things just happen in the best of families. If you are experiencing conflicts and have a desire to change or to make things better, try to remember the following points:

- Keep the lines of communication open.
- Don't expect your sibling to be perfect.
- Stay focused on the issue at hand.
- Learn to talk *with*, not *at* your sibling.
- Realize that ignoring a problem between you will not make it go away.

- Try to use "I" messages instead of "You" messages.
- Express your anger verbally instead of holding it in.

The challenge in sibling relationships should be to develop a sense of pride, closeness, and worthiness among our brothers and sisters. We want to recognize each other's abilities and feel genuine love and concern. Differences of opinion are healthy, and the ability to work out differences is a major feat. A mutually satisfying brother/sister relationship could be summed up in three short sentences:

Make a friend.   Be a friend.   Stay a friend.

CHAPTER 6

Coping with a Substance Abusing Sibling

I n previous chapters we have talked about the different types of conflicts that often occur between brothers and sisters. We have discussed feelings of anger, jealousy, and resentment and heard from teens about their own experiences.

What we have not yet talked about is a situation that is experienced in many families all over the nation. That is the use of drugs or alcohol by one or more siblings.

Perhaps this is occurring in your own household at this very moment. You may be familiar with such feelings as anxiety, mistrust, fear, and hopelessness. Reading what others relate as happening in their own homes may lead you to nod in agreement and say, "I know how it is, I've been there."

When a brother or sister gets involved with alcohol or drugs, the problem does not lie simply with that person. It affects everyone in the family.

Usually, the atmosphere in the home when things are going well is lively and animated. Busy schedules are kept. There are sounds of bickering, sounds of music, TV, and laughter. Siblings quarrel and make up. They share feelings and emotions and often go to other family members for advice and support.

In a home where there is a drug or alcohol problem, true feelings and emotions are not shared. There are secrets. There are lies and deceit and often arguments that end up in physical violence. Children live under great tension and stress. They do not know what will happen from one day to the next. They cannot trust their parents to keep promises, because their parents' attention is turned toward the sibling in trouble.

Consider Mark, a high school junior, whose older brother was and still is an alcoholic.

"Every afternoon coming home from school I would get a tight knot in my stomach. I never knew what to expect from my older brother, who was in high school at the time. If he was just high he was in a fairly good mood, and I could breathe easier. Things were almost normal. But usually by the time I walked in the front door he had been drinking for hours and was really stoned. He was angry and mean when he was drunk. He would chase me through the house yelling and screaming. Mom and Dad were at work until almost dinnertime, so there was no one to protect me. At times he locked me out of the house when it was snowing or raining and very cold. The next day he would apologize and be nice to me. He would call me his buddy and give me what he called a brotherly hug, but I was still afraid of him.

"My brother is in college now and living on campus. I know that he still drinks; I can smell it on him when he comes home. It took me almost a year to feel comfortable walking into my own house after he was gone."

Those of you living with a brother or sister who has a substance abuse problem may be suffering as well. You may be carrying around a tremendous amount of guilt over conflicting feelings. You are angry with your brother for causing the disruption in the family, but how can you say anything about someone who is despondent and in need of help? You hate him for abusing drugs, yet you know that he is helpless to stop himself.

If your sibling is lucky he or she is already enrolled in a treatment program where therapists and counselors can help him or her deal with the problem. If your brother or sister is getting help, he or she has taken an important step toward recovery. He or she has admitted having a substance abuse problem and is letting someone try to help.

Some of you may have a sibling who is not yet at that stage. He or she may still be denying the need for help and denying the existence of a problem. Your sibling may resort to lying, cheating, and stealing and trying every which way to cover up what is happening. You may notice that your sibling tries to keep what is going on a secret. Your parents might decide to go that route also, asking you to keep the secret within the family and not let outsiders know what is happening.

These secrets are difficult to keep, especially when your family is known in the community. People hear, they observe, and they talk. It is also difficult if your sibling attends the same school you do. If your sibling is openly using drugs or alcohol, classmates will see and know what is going on. It's embarrassing. You may feel that others see your sibling's behavior as a reflection on you. Students may say such things as, "What's going on with your sister? Do your parents know that she is on coke? How do you feel about what your sister is doing?" These comments and questions can make you feel terrible and almost wish the two of you weren't related.

Some teens say that they feel caught in the middle. Their sibling asks them to keep his or her habit a secret and not tell their parents. But where does one's allegiance lie? With the sibling who takes you into his or her confidence? Or with your parents, who you know should be told what is going on with their son or daughter?

"In my sophomore year I would pretend that I didn't know my sister, who was a senior. She was in a fast crowd that used crack. She would have mood swings, up one day, down the next. Everyone was talking about her, and it made me feel bad because she was, after all, my sister. I think I mostly felt sorry for her. It was a relief when she graduated and left the school. My junior and senior year were easier. With my sister gone, I could relax and be myself."

A common complaint about a sibling in trouble is that family conversations always seem to revolve around that sibling. "How is Katie feeling today?" "Katie seems depressed; let's talk to her and find out what's wrong." "Katie has an appetite, that's a good sign." But what goes through the other sibling's mind when everyone else seems concerned with Katie?

- I'm not on drugs. Does anyone care about *me* today?
- Is anyone concerned with how I am feeling?
- My grades were up this quarter; does anyone notice?
- There are *two* daughters in this family, or has everyone forgotten?

Some of you may feel sorry for yourself during such a time. You know that your sibling has a problem. He or she is being talked to, reasoned with, counseled. But what about *you*? Who is asking if *you* are scared or anxious about what is happening in the family? Does anyone realize that you are suffering too?

Chances are that during this difficult time there may be no one looking at you or considering your feelings. You may have to fend for yourself and carry on with new strength. Realize that it is only natural for your parents and family to rally around your sibling who is in need of help. If it were you having the problem you would want the same care and attention. But because you are the healthy one and appear to be the strong one, because things may be going well for you during this particular time, you are expected to carry on as you always have.

Your own strength and well-being may not hold up as well as others expect. Many teens interviewed told of times when they were so fed up with their home situation that they considered running away. They were outrageously angry at their sibling for the disruption being caused in the home and angry at their parents too for doing too much or too little.

Some said that their major complaint was the unpredictable atmosphere they had to live in. They never knew what the mood of the family would be from one day to the next.

"If Jonathan was off the booze for a few days, Mom was herself, we'd have breakfast in peace, and I could go to school feeling normal. On his bad days everyone was uptight. Even the dog stayed away, choosing to sleep in a distant corner of the house."

Some of you may have to deal with family plans being canceled at the last minute because of something that has come up with your sibling. The home may be in a constant state of confusion. You want to complain but find yourself holding back because:

- You feel that your parents have enough to worry about without having to listen to you.
- Others might think you are selfish for thinking about yourself during this time.
- Your own complaints would seem so insignificant in comparison to your sibling's.

What do you end up doing? You hold these feelings in and continue to be the helpful son or daughter. Suppressing the feelings after a period of time can cause great tension and stress. You notice a shift in priorities toward your sibling, and you feel somewhat abandoned. Below are some suggestions that might alleviate some of the stressful feelings.

- Try to take one day at a time. Don't feel overwhelmed thinking that there will never be an end to your sibling's problem. Try not to think about what will happen next week or next month or to wonder whether your sibling will be well by a certain date or time.

- Ask your parents if there is anything you can do to help. They may decline, but at least they know and you know that you there for them if needed.
- If you feel a need to talk with someone about your anxieties, confide in a good friend. Sometimes just talking about how you feel to another person, someone you can trust, lifts a burden off your shoulders.
- Don't be afraid to cry if you feel it coming. Crying is a release of pent-up emotions. You will feel a great sense of relief after you have allowed yourself a good cry.
- Let your sibling know that you care and will help if you can, but refuse to lie or steal for him or her.
- You will not be helping your sibling through the crisis.
- Take care of yourself. Get out and visit friends. See movies, be around people. Try to keep your own spirits up by doing pleasant things for yourself.
- Change your expectations of your sibling's behavior during this time. Don't expect him or her to be always cheerful or always talkative and friendly. Realize that this is a difficult time and his or her personality or behavior can be expected to be different.

RECOGNIZING NEGATIVE BEHAVIOR

During this period you will notice changes in your sibling's moods. He or she may be violent one day and meek and apologetic the next, or may sulk for days without speaking. This type of behavior is a symptom of substance abuse. Unfortunately, it affects everyone else in the family as well. Try to understand that much of this negative behavior is temporary and will abate as the problems are worked out.

Try the following exersise. Make a list of all the things your sibling does that make you angry.

- slams doors
- is disrespectful
- is secretive
- is nervous and jumpy

- ties up phone
- screams and yells
- sulks in room
- has mood swings

- lies
- gets abusive
- steals money
- has an eating disorder

Now, cross out each entry on the list that you feel could possibly be attributed to your sibling's problem with drugs or alcohol. Think back to a time when things were going well, before he or she became involved in substance abuse. Did he or she yell and scream, steal money, or have mood swings? Probably not. Chances are that you will be left with but a few items, and that those are things that happen in most well-functioning homes.

Your sibling's behavior while on drugs or alcohol is temporary and will in all likelihood lessen or disappear as he or she gets better. As your sibling's behavior begins to change for the better, your own fears and anxieties will start to lessen also.

How is it in your home? Do you often find yourself:

- Walking around with a nervous stomach, afraid of saying or doing the wrong thing?
- Inventing reasons for friends not to come over for fear of being embarrassed by your sibling's behavior?
- Having to change plans at the last moment due to another problem concerning your sibling?

Realize that you are not alone. But keeping your anger inside and letting it burn can make you act in stressful ways as well. You may say that nothing is wrong but act short and jumpy with your friends or family. Or you may be strangely quiet and feel and act depressed. Suppressing these feelings interferes not only with your own life but with your other relationships as well.

Sometimes it helps to go directly to the source: your sibling. Choose a time that you feel is right, a time when the two of you are alone. Think over what you want to say before you begin speaking. Use a gentle, nonthreatening approach, but don't be afraid to say how his or her behavior is affecting you.

Be prepared for rejection. Your sibling may answer immediately, telling you that it's none of your business. If he or she appears agitated and you see that you will be met with anger, back off and wait for another time. Your sibling may feel that you are interfering where you are not welcome. Don't worsen the situation by trying to force him or her to talk. If, however, you are met with an open or even partially open ear, seize the opportunity. Don't start off by blaming him or her for what is happening.

DESCRIBE WHAT YOU SEE:

- I notice that you've been losing weight lately. You seem rather uptight. Are you feeling okay? Do you want to talk about it?
- I see that you are angry with Mom and Dad. You may not realize it, but they are worried about you. We all are. We want to help.
- I saw you drinking yesterday before you drove Sis to her friend's house. You're putting her life in danger when you drink and drive. I didn't tell Mom or Dad this time, but if it happens again they have to know.
- Have you noticed Tommy and Eva avoiding you lately? They're frightened by the yelling and screaming that is going on around here.

DESCRIBE WHAT YOU FEEL:

- I'm afraid that when you experiment with drugs you will overdose and get seriously ill or die.
- Your outbursts are upsetting the family. We never know what to expect from one day to the next.
- I resent it because Mom and Dad have stopped keeping promises that they made me because of what is going on with you. They always change plans at the last minute, and I'm stuck staying home.
- I'm embarrassed to bring friends home when you've been drinking. I never know how you will act or what kind of mood you will be in.

SHIFT FROM TALKING TO LISTENING

After you have had a chance to describe your feelings to your sibling, give him or her a chance to answer. You may be surprised at the response. He or she may be angry or may ignore you and say nothing. With luck, he or she will take the opportunity to talk about the problem.

Many teens feel more comfortable talking to siblings than to their parents. Perhaps you can pick up a hint as to where your sibling's trouble lies. He or she may confess fears about something that is a complete surprise to the rest of the family. It could be stress over the loss of a girl/boyfriend, or being harassed by a classmate at school. You can learn a lot by listening attentively.

If the lines of communication are open, try not to make judgments or accuse your sibling of wrongdoing. What is not needed at this time is a lecture. What is needed is a friend. If you happen to discover an important clue in something that is said, such as hiding an illness or covering up an eating disorder, ask permission to talk to your parents about it. Your sibling may agree and be relieved to have the secret out in the open. But it could go the other way, and he or she may forbid you to tell your parents.

RECOGNIZING DANGER SIGNS

If your sibling forbids you to go to your parents, you will have to assess the situation. Are there signs of physical illness? Do he or she seem to be covering up an eating disorder, such as anorexia nervosa (starving oneself) or bulimia (binging on food, then forcing oneself to throw up)? Have you seen a bottle of pills or bottles of liquor in the room or somewhere around the house? Have you seen your sibling drinking or taking pills and then driving the car? Has your sibling threatened to run away or commit suicide? Are you aware of your sibling's selling drugs to others, outside the home?

If you answered Yes to any of those questions, it is imperative for you to seek help for your sibling. You must go to your parents, even if told not to. If you feel that you cannot confront them, tell your doctor or teacher or school counselor. By keeping this secret or trying to hide the problem, you will end up hurting your sibling and maybe even the other members of the family. Your sibling could be on a disaster course, heading for jail or possibly death. These are not the kind of secrets that are meant to be kept. It is necessary and permissible to ask others for help.

CHAPTER ◇ 7

Coping with a Sick or Disabled Sibling

J ust as some of you are trying to cope with living with a sibling who abuses drugs or alcohol, so are others living with a physically or mentally ill or disabled sibling. The cause of the illness may have been accident, or it may have been an afflication at birth, such as blindness, cerebral palsy, Down's syndrome, or a neurological problem.

Studies show that children who take part in the care of a disabled sibling tend to become caring and responsible adults. They learn compassion at an early age.

Some of you may have certain responsibilities in the care, such as taking your sibling for a walk in the wheelchair or helping to feed him or her. Besides helping in the daily care, you might read aloud, play games, and be there as a friend. Besides the care and attention, what else do you think you might do to help your sibling feel good about himself or herself?

FOCUS ON SUCCESSES TO BOLSTER CONFIDENCE

We all know what a good feeling it is to be complimented or given a pat on the back for a job well done. It's nice even to hear a few kind words about a personal accomplishment. The same holds true for children who have a physical or mental handicap. Sometimes just a smile or a thumbs up can make a difference if they are struggling with something we may take for granted.

Julian said that his ten-year-old sister, who has Down's syndrome and is mildly retarded, recently mastered writing the alphabet. She had been working for months on writing and memorizing each letter. Julian said that he praised her accomplishments as she made them. He ignored her setbacks and made a big deal out of her progress. Now she is working on numbers and beginning to learn simple addition and subtraction. Julian knows that his praise means a lot to his sister. He plans to continue with his support as she progresses in her lessons.

There are other ways to help build confidence in a disabled sibling. Perhaps your younger sister has just learned to button a shirt or tie a shoe or draw a circle. Stop for a moment and show your enthusiasm. Do not let the opportunity pass. Let her know that you noticed her accomplishment and that you are pleased and excited about it. She may not jump up and give you a detailed explanation of how happy she feels. You may be told with just a smile or a yell or even a quick hug. But that is communication also. It is a major step toward developing her confidence.

Sometimes in living with a disabled sibling you may have questions you are afraid to ask. You wonder what it feels like to be sightless or wheelchair-bound. What does a seizure feel like? How can a deaf person pick up sounds and vibrations? You can imagine your own frustration in wanting to play ball but being unable to because of a physical disability. Try for a moment to put yourself in your brother's shoes. Hear what he hears, see through his eyes. Feel what he feels. You may get upset with him and frustrated with his slowness or inability to complete a task. But if you imagine yourself in his position you may be able to deal with your feelings and be more compassionate.

Sometimes it helps to express your support directly:

- I feel your fear in doing this.
- I understand your frustration in getting this done.
- I can imagine the pain you are feeling.
- I realize your anxiety.

How nice it would be for someone to say this to us during a trying or uncomfortable time, to have someone walk in our shoes and experience what we are experiencing. Somehow it does not seem so awful or frustrating if another person is beside us. It also helps to express positive feelings of support as well:

- I share your joy.
- I feel your excitement.
- I understand your happiness.

Let your sibling know that you are there. Enjoy the closeness and support that your relationship offers.

"Christopher is mildly retarded. He's a great kid. Sometimes I take him along to watch me play soccer. Chris plays soccer in the Special Olympics. I go to watch and cheer for him. I am proud of my brother."

Emilio, 13

"My younger sister Eve has epilepsy. Her seizures are now under control. Once when we were at the library about five years ago, she had a Grand Mal seizure. Mom had taught me what to do if it should happen, and I was prepared. Nobody knows how afraid I am to be alone with my sister. I would never tell her or my mother. It would hurt them, and my mother would think I was terrible because I am healthy and Eve is the one with the problem. This is something I keep hidden inside."

Candy, 15

"My brother has cerebral palsy. He is in a special school for the handicapped. They had a Christmas party at the school a few years ago. I took my friend Noah along. I remember feeling embarrassed for my friend because I saw that he wasn't prepared to meet so many kids in wheelchairs, kids his own age. Some could only breathe with the help of a respirator. I wanted to cut out early, but Noah decided to stay. He helped my brother open his presents, and we didn't leave until the party was over. That night I was angry at myself for feeling embarrassed about my brother. I felt disgusted with myself but grateful to Noah, who is still my friend."

Walter, 16

"It's not easy living with a sibling who has a handicap. Mike was born with brain damage and as a result has severe neurological problems. People stare at him when we go out, but I'm used to it now. Mike likes to be taken out and to be around people rather than stay in the house. I take him to the park, and he watches the kids run around and play on the swings. I understand Mike's needs, and I know he appreciates the help I give him. I think that by being around him I am a better person. I have a lot of patience, and I am strong in the sense that there is not much that makes me turn the other way."

Kelli, 18

Coping with a disabled sibling can be difficult at times, but it can be rewarding as well. You learn compassion and appreciation for the smallest efforts. Many teens interviewed said that they helped with their sibling's physical therapy, such as massaging joints and helping to strengthen weak muscles. They said that it felt good to help with these things. Some said that it made them decide to go into that type of work later, such as a career in medicine or nursing.

It feels good to do for others, but often it is easy to do too much. You mean to do the right thing, but you find yourself performing tasks for your sibling that he or she is capable of doing. Perhaps you notice that you speak on his behalf or answer questions before she has a chance to have her say. How much is too much? How long do you go on helping your brother to feed himself when you know that he is capable of doing it himself? The answer lies with your sibling. If he or she shows a willingness and a desire to do some task, permit it, even if it means it is done wrong or badly the first few times. Let your sibling try to do things on his or her own, without your assistance.

Randi is a fifteen-year-old who found herself doing these very things for her sister, Maxine. Maxine had lost her sight in a boating accident only nine months earlier, and the family was still trying to adjust to the terrible event. Maxine's strength and determination were helping them get through the crisis.

Randi said that at first she tried to do everything for her sister. She was determined to be her sister's eyes. She led Maxine around and told her where everything was and what everything looked like. But it didn't stop there. Randi treated Maxine like a child, making decisions for her, choosing her clothes, and speaking for her when others asked her a question.

At first Maxine was grateful for her sister's help, but as the months wore on she began using a cane and attending a special school to learn to become independent. While Maxine was trying to do things on her own, Randi tried even harder to help. Finally, Maxine explained to Randi that she was doing too much. Maxine told her sister that she appreciated the love and support, but that she wanted to try to do things on her own. She needed to become independent for her own survival.

Dr. Evan Koursh gave his views as a medical professional about those who live with a sick or disabled sibling:

"In the hospital I deal with many sick and dying children and teens. One thing I have found most enlightening is the response on the part of teenagers toward a seriously ill sibling.

"A few years ago I treated a young man with a brain tumor. In the hospital room, he and his older sister fought constantly over what seemed like trivial matters.

"When he was finally diagnosed, their fighting appeared to escalate; she began to act out many of her aggressions toward her brother and her parents.

However, when it was learned that her brother would have to undergo immediate brain surgery, her demeanor changed drastically. She became supportive, caring, and did her best to help her brother through his ordeal. The two actually became closer as a result of his illness. She admitted that she was often jealous of the attention given her brother, but her parents recognized this and tried to make sure that she received 'equal billing'."

FREEDOM OF CHOICE

It is natural to want to look after a sick sibling or to speak on his or her behalf or make choices for him or her. When someone close to you is not as strong or able as you, you want to be a protector. Often, however, your sibling knows exactly what he or she wants or does not want. He enjoys the freedom of making choices just as you do. She wants to be free to choose her friends, clothes, work, or which TV program to watch. When a person has freedom of choice, he or she feels more in control and experiences less stress. Let's face it, nobody likes to be told what to do.

Think about your relationship with your sibling. Do you find yourself:

- Turning to a TV station that you think he would like instead of asking which program he would prefer to watch?
- Buying a treat in a flavor that you think your sister would like instead of finding out her preference?
- Choosing clothes for your brother to get dressed instead of asking him what he would like to wear?
- Answering a question for your sister even though the question was directed at her?

If your sibling shows a desire to think and do for himself or herself, do not underestimate that ability. Help him or her develop the independence of personal choice.

DON'T FORGET ME!

In a home when one sibling is ill or disabled, a great deal of family time and attention goes to that child. He or she receives gifts from sympathetic friends and relatives. It can make the other children feel neglected. Perhaps you have some of these feelings. While you wish only the best for your brother or sister, you feel ornery when the attention is focused on him or her. Some of you may have your own fears and anxieties about your sibling.

- If it can happen to my sister, it can happen to me.
- My brother is so dependent on me. I can never let him down.
- What right do I have to be happy when my sister suffers so much?

You may even shy away from family participation or shut yourself away from the rest of the family Realize that by doing this you only give yourself more time to feel sorry for yourself and to harbor these thoughts. If you find yourself sulking and feeling down, try doing the following:

- Put your thoughts into words. It will help to ease your anxieties. Discuss your feelings with your parents or even your sibling if he or she is able to understand.
- Get involved and give of yourself. Ask your parents, "How can I help you today?"
- Offer to take over some of the responsibilities of

caring for your sibling. When you are busy doing for others, you tend to forget to feel sorry for yourself.

The stress you may feel in coping with a disabled brother or sister is categorized as a healthy kind of stress. It is the kind that builds character and brings the family closer together. In her book *Stress and the Healthy Family,** Dolores Curran writes: "Healthy families recognize that stresses are a means of identifying family strengths. When a family experiences stress, it is tested as a unit and learns to use its strengths and resources."

Dealing with or just coping with sick or disabled siblings is okay, but in most cases it is not enough. These are people who need you as no other person will ever need you again. Be there for them! Go that extra step. Try to think of yourself in terms of action verbs: *give—feel—express—assist—involve—understand.*

Continue to be a source of love and compassion and caring and you will get back double the effort you expend.

* Harper & Row, New York, 1985.

CHAPTER 8

Strengthening

Sibling Bonds

"I can fight with my parents, my cousins, and my friends and still keep my self-control, with almost anyone except my brothers. I think it's because they know me better than anyone else. We bunk together, we eat meals together, we go to the same school. They know what makes me happy and they also know which buttons to press to make me explode in anger. I think my siblings know me about as well as I know myself, and that's pretty close. It's hard to lie to a brother who knows every facial expression. You can't escape it; they are blood and the connection is permanent—it's for keeps."

Jesse, 17

How true that is. Sibling bonds, good ones or bad ones, close or distant, are difficult to put aside or ignore. They run deeper than friendship.

When you love a sibling, however, you do not love him

or her all the time, in exactly the same way. You may go for days without speaking to your brother or sister, but after the air has cleared you become close once again. Each day is different, with good moods, bad moods, pleasant and unpleasant experiences occurring between you.

Some sibling relationships falter and may go on a downswing for years, such as the sister who wrote to Ann Landers describing their lifelong grudge. But many brother/sister relationships are sustained throughout the years.

Your siblings are usually the first people besides your parents to come to your aid in time of trouble. They know your admirable qualities, they know your faults. They've seen you during the good times, but they've also seen you at your very worst.

Those of you currently involved in a bitter sibling relationship may be wishing for things to get better, but deep down inside you feel they never will. You may feel that this is the way it will always be, with your sibling bossing you around or with you feeling envious over what he or she has or how he or she looks. Perhaps you feel, as many do, that your sibling wishes you were different and is trying to change you into a person that you are not.

Realize that no one can boss you around or change you without your consent. You don't have to sit back and take ridicule or insults. There are alternatives to fighting back that do not involve violence, as we have discussed. Remember that unresolved hurt and anger lie waiting for trivial incidents to bring them out in the open again. When feelings are not shared, you feel lonely and resentful.

It is important, then, to express your hurt or anger and not wait for it to build up. If your brother or sister seems willing to talk, take the initiative and begin a conversation. Be happy for the discussion, even if you feel somewhat embarrassed or uneasy about it.

Show your sibling in actions that you respect and admire him or her and that you really do enjoy the opportunity to share experiences.

Above all, try to be a good listener. If your brother or sister feels down and needs an ear to complain to or a shoulder to cry on, be there for him or her. By taking an interest in his or her problems you show that you care and that when the chips are down you can be counted on.

"My brother and sister were on their own when I was in my teens. I have had very little to do with my brother, mostly because of geography. My family was mostly dominated by my mother, who tried to run everyone and everything. The fact that I was happily married for forty-two years was a result of my not allowing my mother to run me or my family. My brother and sister were each divorced twice, and it makes me sure that I made the right decision. Looking back, pre-adult, we were quite a happy family."

Maurie, 71

"I have a sister who is fourteen. I live out here in California and she's back East still living with my parents. I kind of worry about her even though she's with my parents. We didn't play together when we were growing up. She had her friends, school, and I had mine. Because I was the oldest I think my parents made mistakes with me first, like with rules. They were easier with her than with me. I wouldn't say she was babied; it's just that I got a lot of, 'Your sister is younger than you, so don't do this or that to her'."

David, 21

"I was always treated like a baby, and babies do not contribute worthwhile solutions. Because of this my life has always been insecure and fear-dominated, something I am now working on."

Rose, 48

"Being from older parents, when I was born they believed in children doing as they were told. It was a dictatorship. There were no conflicts as long as I went along with their wishes.

Never having had brothers or sisters, it has been hard for me to understand that siblings are not always close just because they are brother and sister and that many brothers and sisters grow up and actually do not like one another and never see each other. My picture of 'families' was of a big, happy family, so when my own children argue or fight and do not get along, it is hard for me to understand and to know how to help them resolve their differences.

I believe having brothers and sisters teaches you how to get along with different types of people. It also teaches you to stand up and fight for yourself. You miss out on these lessons as an only child. Everything is planned around an only child; you and your parents have no one else to consider."

Myra

"This year when my sister and I got our new school clothes we both promised not to take each other's things without asking, and so now we don't fight about that anymore. We even signed a paper so we have proof of our agreement."

Jennifer, 13

"In looking back on our relationship, the first thing I realized was that although I had always been an understanding and caring person with my friends, as soon as my sister started to talk to me about something I seemed to turn off. It was as if an automatic switch shut down my ears and the communication between us.

By the time I realized this, I must have been doing it for years, and it took a real effort to break out of the unconscious action. I made a real effort to focus and to listen to my sister. After a while it became easier, more natural and more interesting. The more I listened, the more she listened and the more we got to know each other and become genuinely interested in each other's lives."

Laurie, 21

"If I have a conflict with one of my brothers, Mom and Dad don't know about it because we either work it out or it doesn't happen in front of them. If it's serious, like if we display anger or stop talking to each other, Mom notices that something's up, and then she takes one of us aside and talks to us separately and tries to explain the other's feelings.

That usually works because she'll tell me things that I didn't realize and I'll look at the problem differently. I like that better because my brother does say things that hurt me. I still remember those things today and they still hurt. I don't know if he feels the same way."

Amy, 16

"When I was younger and my sister and I would get into a fight, my parents would get real bent out of shape. Whatever we were fighting over, my parents (in a very angry way) would make sure that neither of us got what we were fighting over, and we would usually lose some other privilege on top of it. I guess they showed us.

My sister and I were so afraid to fight, or even to disagree, that when something came up we would just stuff our feelings and get real resentful instead.

That might have something to do with why my brothers and sisters and I never really worked through anything together, and today I still feel rather far away from them.

James

"I fight with Mom, mostly about my room or about doing chores. My sister Jenny and I fight a lot, but we make up fast because we don't like to be mad and we have to be together a lot because we share a bedroom.

If we are in a fight, Mom and Dad make us go to our room and talk everything out before we are allowed to come out. We fight a lot because Jenny weighs more than me and she wears my clothes and pops buttons on my pants.

Mom makes us talk about what is bothering us, and sometimes I feel better, but not always. Sometimes I just want to be by myself when I am mad, and most of the time she doesn't let me."

Rosalie

The above contributors are in all probability dealing with some of the very same problems that you have. As you can see, many of the differences involve parents and how they react to the rivalry among their children.

It is important for parents to realize that each child is different. If they try to treat all their children alike, it denies their uniqueness. Fairness does not always diminish sibling rivalry. Moms and Dads should recognize and respect their kids' differences.

Fighting is normal. Many experts agree that the absence

of sibling rivalry can be a sign of trouble. They promote the encouragement of healthy competition where brothers and sisters can release hidden frustrations.

Whether your sibling is younger or older than you, the age difference means less than the bonds that connect you. Your little brother won't always be a pest as he grows older. Your relationship will change, and as adults you may end up looking to him for support and advice.

"But I can't help feeling jealous or envious of my sibling," you may be saying. Remember that jealousy is a natural and normal emotion. Everyone who cares and loves feels jealous at one time or another. You have to decide whether you will allow your jealousy to get in the way of your relationship or accept it as a natural part of your personal growth.

If you feel that you are jealous or envious of a brother or sister, try to recognize exactly what it is that bothers you. Read over Chapter 4 on Jealousy and try to use what was said.

Besides feeling jealous, ask yourself the following: When you have had a bad day with your sibling, with teasing, insults, and so on, what feeling dominates? How open are each of you in admitting hurt, anger, or responsibility? Do you yell at each other? Do you hold a grudge? Do you become silent or act overly sensitive? Try to see your own reaction as your sibling sees it.

Many parents have tried the experiment of keeping a tape recorder on throughout the day to record their conversations with their children. How surprised many of them were to hear the sound of their own angry voices, their shouting of commands to their kids. Imagine yourself speaking during an altercation with your siblings. What do you think they would see or hear? You may be antagonizing them just by the tone of your voice or the way you stand. If you come at them with an angry face and clenched fists before you begin speaking, they will probably take the defensive immediately. Try to approach the problem calmly and give them a chance to explain their side.

Realize also that most sibling fights are the result not of disagreement, but of poor communication. Communication is composed of talking and listening. Unfortunately, brothers and sisters often fail to say clearly what they feel, need, and want of each other. Keep those lines of communication open. By doing so you can exchange an understanding of what hurts you and what makes them angry, and then try to correct whatever misunderstandings still exist.

Yes, it is okay to get angry and to disagree with someone you love. If you can't get angry at your sibling, your relationship is not real. No one goes through every day with a grin and a happy attitude toward a sibling. You can't feel close to or trust someone at whom you can't get angry. Most families have arguments and conflicts, tears and harsh words said in the heat of anger. That is part of human nature.

Get to know your sibling better through what each of you feels. Your brothers and sisters are the few people whom you will allow to be close enough to share your deepest concerns, your fears, and your decisions about life in general. Underneath fancy clothes, makeup, guarded exteriors, lies a unique individual, the someone your sibling knows and understands—*you*.

Much, if not most, of our capacity to form trusting relationships is rooted in the early stages of life. By knowing this, and by learning from the foregoing chapters, you have a head start. Enjoy this beginning phase of a rich and lifelong sibling relationship.

If you currently harbor bad feelings toward a sibling,

decide today that you will make a real effort to work things out. Precious time is wasted in relationships that are damaged by holding grudges or by deliberately ignoring one another. When things begin to get better, you will see that your renewed bonds are those of shared courage and true friendship. Learning to forgive and forget and to start anew takes bravery and trust. The rewards are worth the risk.

CHAPTER 9

Questions and

Answers from a Pro

D. Joy Gould has many years of experience in working with adolescents and their families in numerous problem areas, including abuse of drugs and alcohol. She is Director of Outpatient Services for the Los Angeles Centers for Alcohol and Drug Abuse and is a professor at Pacific Oaks College in Pasadena, teaching courses on counseling. Here she answers a few key questions on sibling problems.

Q. From a professional point of view, can you suggest to teenagers how they can learn to live with sibling quarrels—not just everyday disagreements, but fighting that goes on and often explodes into major battles, leaving physical and emotional scars?

A. In working with teens I regularly hear about nagging issues that don't seem to change:

- Sara always borrows my favorite clothes without asking.

- Paul is always on the phone when I need it.
- Amy steals all my friends away from me.
- Gary constantly picks on me about my hair, my clothes, everything.

Each issue by itself can be painful. Unfortunately, in relationships with brothers and sisters problems often come together to become overpowering. The result is a buildup of resentment, anger, and frustration at being unable to change the situation. The anger is directed at the sibling, but it is also directed inward.

As problems mount between brothers and sisters, arguments become bitter, and resentment can be held for a long time, even into adulthood.

In talking to teens, I tell them that they have choices about how to deal with these problems. First and most important, they must recognize and understand what it is that their brother or sister does that hurts them. Next they must recognize how it makes them feel.

They know that fighting back or trying to ignore the situation has not helped, so the only choice is to try something different. I recommend taking action immediately, not letting the situation go on without trying to change it. Using the examples given above, they might handle the situations this way:

- "Sara, when you borrow my clothes I feel frustrated and angry. I want you to stop doing it without asking permission."
- "Paul, when you use the phone so much I feel angry that I am not getting my turn. I want you to share the phone. Maybe one way would be to limit the time on each call."
- "Amy, when my friends come over you manage to get all their attention, and I'm left out. That makes

me feel sad and angry. I want you to let me have time alone with my friends."

- "Gary, when you tease me about my clothes and my hair I feel hurt and angry. I want you to put yourself in my place. How would you like to have someone always saying you're not OK?"

In these examples the brother or sister told the sibling that one thing he or she did created a certain feeling. It may be news to the sibling. The brother or sister also stated what he or she would like the sibling to do. If you do not ask for what you want from others, there is no possibility of getting it.

Making an attempt to handle each situation as it arises can stop the buildup of anger and resentment. The most important thing teens can do to effect change with a brother or sister is to open up the lines of communication, to be direct and clear about what they want and how they feel.

Q. Can you give some insight into the effect of birth order—where a child stands in the family? How can younger brothers or sisters hold their ground against older siblings who boss them around? How can older siblings deal with always having to take care of younger ones?

A. I believe that personality traits are formed very early in families. I do not place much emphasis on birth order in assessing individual or family problems.

The kinds of problems faced by children depend largely on how their parents intereact with them, the expectations the parents have of each child, and the demands they make on them.

Children may get stuck in a certain role because of their parents' treatment and be unable to break out of that mold, even into adulthood.

I cannot overemphasize the need for open communication in families. So often hurt feelings or resentment build
up because of lack of communication. For example:

- Penny is sixteen and often is required to baby-sit for
  her younger brother and sister. Penny is bossy with
  them, and they are unhappy about her treatment.
  Penny is angry at always having to take care of the
  younger kids.

Penny should talk with her parents about her resentment
of baby-sitting. While communicating her anger about it,
she should also ask for what she wants. That may be to
baby-sit less frequently or not at all. If communication is
open in her family, her parents will probably compromise.
Penny may then be less bossy with the younger children
because she feels less angry.

Her brother and sister also have a role here. They need
to talk with Penny and express how they feel about her
bossiness. They should also state what they would like from
Penny, which may be for her to be more like a sister than a
third parent. That may bring about some change in Penny.

Communication about a problem is the only way to effect
change. If you feel stuck in a certain role within the family,
talk it through. When people are aware of your true feelings,
an effort may be made to respond differently.

Q. Many teens admit that much of their rivalry stems
from feelings of jealousy and favoritism in the family. One
sister may be an honor student and receive parental praise
and attention, or a brother may be a television actor and
seem to have all the friends. Often the other sibling feels
left out, and feelings of anger arise. How can he or she cope
with these feelings?

A. Jealousy and envy are normal reactions when parents,

teachers, or other respected adults show favoritism for one child. If one sister receives more gifts, the other feels left out, unloved, not OK. It is easy then to wonder whether he or she is important enough to deserve praise or gifts or attention. His or her own value in the world becomes a big question. Meanwhile, resentment and even hatred may arise toward the favored brother or sister.

None of these feelings are wrong. It is important for teens to know that feelings are just that: feelings. They are neither right nor wrong. What is harmful is not expressing those feelings.

Coping with jealous feelings requires first of all acknowledging that they exist and saying, "OK, this is how I feel." Identifying the problem becomes important. A former client of mine, Jon, who is fourteen, said:

- "My brother Adrian is a football star. Everybody thinks he's great. When he's around no one notices me."

Is Adrian the problem? No, not really. Adrian didn't ask for the attention. What Adrian did was to excel in something he liked to do, and he received recognition for it.

Is Jon at fault? No, Jon has done nothing to make people not notice him.

What about the people who are ignoring Jon? They are not ignoring him intentionally; they are acknowledging Adrian.

Since no one is really doing anything intentional to Jon, what can Jon do? He can do several things. He, like everyone else, is concentrating on Adrian. Jon is fully aware of how special Adrian is. Jon can focus his attention on Jon. He can explore his own strengths and areas of accomplishment. That will help him have a more positive self-image. Making a list of those positive things can help. Also, by acknowledging himself and building up his self-esteem Jon may develop the courage to communicate some of the negative feelings he has been carrying.

My advice always is to express these feelings, particularly to someone who is trustworthy. If Jon can discuss the problem with his parents, all the better. Jon's parents may not have been aware that they paid more attention to Adrian and that this affected Jon. Knowing the situation can allow them to demonstrate their feelings of pride in the child they have not been acknowledging.

One of the hardest lessons to learn in a family and in life is that things are not fair and people are not always treated equally. Sometimes the family may not provide all the love and caring that each member needs. It may become necessary to look to friends and other adults for respect, caring, and acceptance. Even so, we may not always be able to depend on others to praise us for our good qualities. Each person must develop a way of loving himself or herself.

Q. Many teems are living in a home situation in which a brother or sister is involved with drugs or alcohol. When should a sibling break the confidence of a brother or sister who is headed for trouble?

A. Living with a brother or sister who uses drugs or alcohol or sells drugs is a serious problem. Teens are much concerned about what to do with the knowledge. The most common feelings expressed to me are:

- Guilt because of hiding the truth.
- Fear of retaliation by the sibling.
- Fear for the safety of the drinker/user/seller.

Teenagers start using drugs or alcohol because everyone else is doing it or because they want to stay in the right crowd. Trying drugs or alcohol is often done just to find out what it is like.

Putting aside the matter of curiosity, it is important to remember that in the United States it is illegal to buy alcohol under the age of eighteen or twenty-one, depending on the state. Drugs are illegal at any age. So a brother or sister involved with alcohol is in serious trouble to begin with, having broken the law.

Often teens are not much concerned with the legal angle. Most often the question is how much is too much. At what point should a brother or sister be concerned. As a rule of thumb, if you ask that question, you already know that there is a problem. We do not ask questions that have no meaning in our lives.

The questions below are used by professionals to determine whether or not a drug or alcohol problem exists. They can be used as a guide to decide whether a brother or sister has crossed the line from experimenting with drugs or alcohol to becoming dependent on them.

	Yes	No
• Does he or she lose time from school because of drinking or using drugs?	___	___
• Does he or she use drugs or drink alone?	___	___
• Does he or she borrow money or "do without" other things to buy liquor or drugs?	___	___
• Has his or her group of friends changed?	___	___
• Have friends said that he or she drinks or uses drugs too much?	___	___
• Does his or her personality change when drinking or using drugs?	___	___

A "Yes" answer to two or more questions can mean that a brother or sister needs the help of the entire family. By not sharing this knowledge, which is weighing heavily on the one who knows, that person is allowing the drug user or drinker to become more deeply involved in his or her problem. Parents must be informed, even though the drug user or drinker may retaliate. By sharing the knowledge, even though sworn to secrecy, the sibling may save a life.

Q. How can siblings cope with living with a sick or disabled brother or sister?

A. Coping with the problems of living with a brother or sister who is ill puts a great strain on everyone in the family. The sibling who is ill gets the attention of the whole family because of his or her physical needs. For the brother or sister who is well the result may be:

• Feeling abandoned or left out.
• Feeling in the way.
• Feeling guilty about being well.
• Feeling resentment and possibly hatred for the ill sibling.
• Fearing the disease and possibly contracting it.

Living with the family illness may require accepting the fact that the family cannot be as loving and caring to the well child. Don't stop there. Seek love, affection, and approval from outside sources, from people outside the immediate family. But don't give up on the family. Communicate your needs and fears, especially fears about the disease. Ask for information. If parents cannot give a clear explanation, ask the family doctor.

Some teens feel that the way to get attention is to be ill or become ill. That is not a positive way to cope with feeling left out. The brother or sister with a disease did not make the choice, nor did the family ask for the problem. Such problems occur, and each member must try to cope in the best way possible.

Many teens want to help, but parents won't allow them that opportunity. Don't give up. Ask to be given some responsibilities, no matter how small—perhaps cooking a special meal or reading aloud. Let parents know that helping will help you, too.

Bibliography

Al-Anon Family Group. *Hope for Children of Alcoholics*. New York: Al-Anon Headquarters, 1982.

Arnstein, Helene S. *Brothers and Sisters*. New York: E.P. Dutton, 1979.

Atkins, Dale V. *Sisters*. New York: Arbor House, 1984.

Banks, Stephen P., and Kahn, Michael D. *The Sibling Bond*. New York: Basic Books, 1987.

Barun, Ken. *How to Keep the Children You Love Off Drugs*. New York: Atlantic Monthly Press, 1988.

Bower, Sharon Anthony, and Gordon H. *Asserting Yourself*. Reading, MA: Addison Wesley, 1976.

Faber, Adele. *Brothers and Sisters*. New York: W. W. Norton, 1987.

Fishel, Elizabeth. *Sibling Rivalry*. New York: William Morrow, 1979.

Friday, Nancy. *Jealousy*. New York: William Morrow, 1985.

Howard, Jane. *Families*. New York: Simon & Schuster, 1978.

Kagan, Jerome. *Twelve to Sixteen: Early Adolescence*. New York: W.W. Norton, 1972.

Leman, Kevin. *The Birth Order Book*. New York: Dell Publishers, 1985.

Meehan, Bob. *Beyond the Yellow Brick Road*. New York: Contemporary Books, 1984.

North, Robert. *Teenage Drinking*. New York: Macmillan, 1980.

Novotny, Pamela Patrick. *The Joy of Twins*. New York: Crown, 1988.

Pearlman, Laura, and Scott, Kathleen Anton. *Raising the Handicapped Child*. Englewood Cliffs, NJ.: Prentice-Hall, 1981.

Reit, Seymour V. *Sibling Rivalry.* New York: Random House, 1985.

Tannen, Deborah. *That's Not What I Meant!* New York: William Morrow, 1983.

Index